NINJA AIR FRYER COOKBOOK UK

2000 Days of Delicious, Quick & Easy Ninja Air Fryer Recipes for Beginners and Advanced Users

BY OLIVER WEST

Disclaimer and Terms of Use:

Effort has been made to ensure that the information in this book is accurate and complete, however, the author and the publisher do not warrant the accuracy of the information, text and graphics contained within the book due to the rapidly changing nature of science, research, known and unknown facts and internet. The Author and the publisher do not hold any responsibility for errors, omissions or contrary interpretation of the subject matter herein. This book is presented solely for motivational and informational purposes only.

TABLE OF CONTENTS

DESSERTS 91

INTRODUCTION

Welcome to the Ninja Air Fryer Cookbook!

If you have finally bought a Ninja Air Fryer or are planning to buy one, then you need to give yourself a break and cook some of the finest dishes to try this fantastic machine out. This book walks you through the simplest route to take. No need to worry about your hectic routine and spend time looking for recipes, as this cookbook will help you sort out most things with no trouble.

Did you ever wonder why, out of so many electronic appliances, an air fryer is so in demand among people of all ages? There must be some amazing benefits to this machine that can't be ignored, like saving time and making sure that people get the right meals in the best way possible.

Nowadays, everyone is in a hurry, and people don't like to spend time on time-consuming meals. Either they prefer to order from their favourite fast-food chain or look for ways to cook meals that require less time. If you are one of those people, you have landed in the right place. An air fryer is all you need to leave your worries behind, because now you can have enough time to do your day-to-day chores and work on the pending assignment without fussing around.

When it comes to cooking, one can't limit themselves to a few fixed options to prepare certain dishes. Contrary to popular belief, you can make the most out of a Ninja Air Fryer by flexing your culinary skills. The sky's the limit, so put yourself at ease as now, with the help of this book, you have unlimited ways and options to explore and impress your guests on special occasions.

This cookbook gives you a complete introduction to the Ninja Air Fryer. It doesn't matter what's on the menu; you'll cook like a pro without spending much time. The Ninja Air Fryer Cookbook has all the best features a beginner should know about. You can learn everything you are supposed to know about your favourite machine with a comprehensive overview of its functions.

Get ready to prepare, regardless of the type, whether you are looking forward to making a well-prepared breakfast, lunch, or dinner or need to prepare appetizers and desserts. Just entertain your friends and family with your cooking skills, with the added spice of cooking in this perfect Ninja Air Fryer. Just spice up your cooking expertise with this easy-to-use cooking appliance and boost the nutritional value of your daily meals. Cooking was never easier before the Ninja Air Fryer, as you can save time and energy with easy-to-prepare recipes in no time.

ABOUT THIS BOOK

If you are a foodie, you must be tempted to eat some unique meals at different times of the day or night. It doesn't matter if you are craving something, but how much time it would take to prepare that meal matters a lot because most of the time, you would like to cook something that can be done instantly. Don't worry; this book was written with today's nutritional concerns about unhealthy eating, cooking styles, and ways to save time when cooking in mind.

Apart from the detailed description of the meals, you will find out the perks of using the Ninja with no trouble air fryer, why it is so much in demand, and the best ways people can use it. Not only that, but you will also learn some tips and tricks through which you can prepare your favourite meals at any time you want. The extensive research that has been done while writing this book says a lot about the recipes and the ingredients of the dishes that are listed here.

When you have a Ninja Air Fryer cookbook, you will always have options and variations for preparing your daily meals. There is nothing that this book can't help you with. Try out some original recipes in a range of cuisines that you would love to cook with the help of this book. This cookbook is a step-by-step guide to your regular meals, and it doesn't even matter what you feel like eating, as it has a variety of recipes enlisted here for your ease, so you can cook whatever you feel like anytime you want. Whether you are cooking for vegetarians or non-vegetarians, you will find several options to choose from based on your preferences.

With the help of a multi-tasking Ninja Air Fryer cookbook, everything can go smoothly, especially if you are looking into low-calorie recipes. Along with the numerous dishes, you will find all the ingredients, the time that is taken while preparing the meals, and their nutritional value, so all those people who are concerned about their meals and how many calories they are consuming daily would love to try out this book as it has sorted out everything for the sake of your convenience.

WHAT IS THE NINJA AIR FRYER?

Ninja is a well-known company making home appliances such as fryers, blenders, and ovens. Their products are of high quality, and even though most are made of plastic, they are made of solid and durable material. They are easy to clean, and some products come with unique attachments and accessories, such as a food processor or micro juicer. When we talk about Ninja air fryers, they are a popular choice for those who are into cooking regularly at home and professional chefs because of the product's versatility, ease of usage, and productivity.

Finding the correct air fryer by keeping in mind one's needs, budget, and preferences can be daunting when the market has so many options to pick from and everyone claims to be the best one. Still, with the Ninja air fryer, everything can go smoothly as long as it has the right combination of operationality and efficiency. Ninja's air fryers come with a compact model for your small kitchen or a larger unit for amusement; they will get you covered in all setups. You can use their fryers for perfectly cooked, low-calorie French fries and crispy, tender chicken wings that make you feel like they have come straight out of the deep fryer.

This is one of many ways you can use a Ninja Air Fryer, as there are other ways of cooking meals, like if you need to prepare something soggy, like chewy cookies that come along with a nice coating of golden edges without making them too crispy. In terms of functioning, the control panel of these fryers is highly intuitive; the digital screen describes the various functions, so users don't have to guess and play around. To make it work, choose the function you'd like to go for, and then you can manually toggle to increase temperature and time. The drawer is easy to take out and is light enough to carry different kitchen items.

The basket and insert are dishwasher-safe, which makes them easy to wash. Their handles can be grabbed easily, and the drawer is intuitive, so it can be pulled out to check out meals or give them a shake. These air fryers are very easy to set up and need minimal unpacking. You need to remove them from the box and remove any plastic or cardboard covering from the outside or inside of the fryer. Then wash the basket once before you use it, and plug it in. You can easily choose from the functions on the control panel. Before placing any food, the instructions refer to preheating it for 3 minutes.

HOW DOES THE NINJA AIR FRYER FUNCTION?

Air fryers utilize convection heat when cooking meals so that they are browned and crispy on the outside but stay slightly wet and soft on the inside. Cooking with a Ninja air fryer requires less time and makes less of a mess than deep-frying or traditional oven roasting. Oil is used sparingly when using a Ninja Air Fryer.

Ninja air fryers come with perforated baskets, wire racks, and ceramic plates that have holes in them and let hot air from above circulate food at temperatures around 400 degrees Fahrenheit (204°C). All of this prepares the outside of the meal first and seals in the moisture. In case you're looking for ease of usage, you'll find that some Ninja fryer models come with preset programs to prepare regular meals with the touch of a single button.

Ninja fryers that are basket-style or single-zone have cooking baskets just like those in traditional deep fryers and are big enough to roast a 3-pound chicken. There are some known as "dual-zone air fryers," which let users cook two foods at different temperatures and cook times, utilizing smart finish technology to make sure that they are completed simultaneously.

The terms single- and dual-zone indicate the device's number of individual cooking chambers. Some of these units also contain racks when users need more space between items, like when preparing chicken breasts or dehydrating fruits.

Always remember that you'll have to ensure that there is enough space between items so there can be proper air circulation. You'll get bad results if you put too much in the basket or on the racks. Overfilling will result in mushy or unevenly cooked food. It is best to pay attention to the size and shape of the cooking area and the whole dimensions of the portion while choosing one that suits your preferences in the best way possible.

Following are some steps for using a Ninja Air Fryer, so look and find out how it works.

Placing Food in the Basket

It is based on the air fryer's size; the basket can hold anywhere from 2 to 10 quarts. Most of the time, you'll have to include 1 or 2 teaspoons of oil to help the food get nice and crispy. If you're in a hurry, you can keep the foil in an air fryer to facilitate cleanup.

Setting Time and Temperature

Usually, an air fryer's cooking time and temperature range from 5 to 25 minutes at 350°F (177°C) to 400°F (204°C), based on the food you are preparing, so always make sure of the temperature at which it needs to be cooked for a particular dish.

Allow the Meal to be Cooked

At times, users need to flip or turn the food halfway while they are cooking it to help it crisp up properly. When you are done cooking, it's important to clean the air fryer.

PERKS OF USING A NINJA AIR FRYER

Below are some perks associated with Ninja air fryers that users should know about.

Ease of Usage

The air fryer came to the surface as a statement for a deep fryer. Even though that was a good choice, it wasn't enough to get most people to pick it because deep-frying wasn't something they did often. Everyone is busy these days, and even if people love to cook, they have less time for it because there are various other things to do first.

That is why already-cooked meals and takeaways are so in demand, even when people know how unhealthy they are. Here, Ninja air fryers come in handy, and preparing your favourite meals at home sounds more convenient.

This air fryer makes the task of cooking your regular meals uncomplicated. You need to take out a piece of meat, like a chicken breast (even frozen meat will serve the purpose), place it in the basket, and set it to cook, as everything will be done instantly.

Easy to Clean

Ninja's Air Fryer is incredibly easy to clean after you use it. If you clean it after each use, it will only need regular cleaning, just like any other pot or pan you've used. Just put soapy water in the basket and use a sponge that won't scratch to clean the inside or outside. Some of these air fryer baskets can go in the dishwasher.

You can also give the whole unit, including the cooking coil, a deeper clean about once or twice a month, depending on how often you use it. It will be easier than it sounds if you do it on a daily basis.

Faster as Compared to Oven Cooking

One of the main perks of using a Ninja Air Fryer is that it gets very hot very quickly, and the circulating air helps the food cook properly and get browned and crispy without much interference from your end. This means users will be able to cut their cooking time. An air fryer is faster than an oven in terms of cooking, not just because it can get hot quickly but because of the smaller size of the air fryer compared to the oven.

An oven usually requires 10 minutes to pre-heat, and the air fryer doesn't require any pre-heating time for most recipes. This means that users can place their food right into the basket, slide it into the air fryer, arrange the time, and get ready to eat in 10-15 minutes. It's an incredible tool in case You are looking for solutions that can help you make quick and easy snacks. It doesn't matter if this is for a party or after-school treats; using an air fryer is extremely easy. Place in your favourite snack and cook it within minutes.

TIPS FOR COOKING
IN THE NINJA AIR FRYER

Are you looking for some ways to get your hands on some of the best cooking techniques for a Ninja Air Fryer? If yes, the tips below will help you learn all about it, so find out and know how this will work.

1. Add Minimal Oil

While cooking, it is recommended not to add too much oil. Foods that are being prepared in the Ninja Air Fryer only require a little oil to crisp them up. If you have added extra oil, it will simply drip from the food and pool at the bottom of the fryer, causing smoke.

You need to spray foods with a bit of a mist of oil. Apart from that, there is no need to include additional oil in frozen deep-fried foods because they already have a lot of oil in the bread. Vegetables benefit from being lightly oiled. Chicken thigh pieces don't need any oil.

2. Avoid Misting Oil with Food

Take the food from the fryer to safely include oil or cooking spray in your dish. Always spray the meal with cooking spray when it is out of the machine, as most of these sprays can cause a sticky buildup on the internal surfaces of the air fryer. This can be done by removing your meal from the fryer and adding a proper oil coating.

3. Adding Extra Shake

Most models of Ninja air fryers suggest users remove the cooking basket and mix it once or twice while the cooking is in progress. But it is recommended that one always add an extra shake. Just mix it more than is required in case you need crispy and properly browned results.

4. Cooking Time is not Fixed

While using any fryer, cooking time can't be fixed. There is always a chance that you will have to prepare for more or less time than a recipe requires. Always keep checking the food and be ready for any changes, as 2 to 5 minutes notice can always be expected.

5. Avoid Overcrowding the Basket

It is always recommended not to stuff food in the basket because it will ruin it. Food requires space and air circulation to get crispy in the air fryer. If you fill it with a whole bag of frozen fries, they won't get as crispy as you expect. Apart from that, it will take more time to cook.

6. Check the Temperature while Cooking

People say that meat should be cooked the right way to kill bacteria, and sometimes the crispiness that comes from air-frying can hide the fact that meat wasn't cooked enough. It is better to check the temperature while you are cooking to see whether or not it is done, especially when preparing steak, pork, and chicken. The best safe-to-eat meat should be cooked at 145 degrees Fahrenheit (63°C), including pork, beef, lamb, and ground meats, like pork beef, which should reach 160 degrees Fahrenheit (71°C); all poultry should be cooked at 165 degrees Fahrenheit (74°C).

7. Using Tin Foil

Tin foil can be used in the air fryer to keep the food from sticking and to make cleanup easier. You can also wrap liquid foods in it or steam your meal. An aluminium pan can also be used, which also works fine in the air fryer. Disposable foil pans can be the best way to reheat meals in the air fryer, such as casseroles or lasagna.

8. Soak Sliced Bread in Grease.

Ninja fryers are good for the environment because users can switch from aluminium foil liners to a slice of bread that can be thrown away. You can place a piece of bread on the surface of your air fryer. It's like going green with the option to use foil for catching grease and drips for effortless clean-up. You can also limit food waste and use this method to prepare greasy foods such as bacon and stale bread slices.

9. Preparing Foil for Crumbed Meals

If your Ninja Air Fryer has a wire rack instead of a solid base, it is recommended that you lay down a layer of foil or a specially-made air fryer liner before preparing a crumbed meal or sticky foods. This will make sure that the coating isn't rubbed off during the process of shaking, and it will also make cleaning a bit easier. The only thing you are supposed to ensure is that the foil only covers the base of the basket partially, and you need the air to flow from under the basket. There is no need to let the foil come up over the meal near the element and fan.

10. Removing the Basket Before Dumping

Most basket-style air fryers come in two pieces. There's the drawer and the basket that snaps into it. It's best to take the whole cradle out of the air fryer and take out the food; doing so can be the reason why all the remaining oil on the surface also comes out. It is best to remove the basket before you are about to take the food out.

11. Add Water to the Drawer while Preparing Fatty Meals

When preparing high-fat foods such as bacon or chicken wings, grease can be an integral part of the cooking process and the source of messes and foul odours. It is suggested to include some water on the surface of the drawer, in case the design allows it before you are about to cook, to stop the fat from smoking. or by using a liner designed for air-frying to reduce the mess.

12. Avoid Cooking Light Meals

"Light" means something that is nearly weightless. If you add something to the air fryer that is too light, it will fly off and melt into the surface of the cradle. It doesn't mean that you can't prepare something soft, so keep an eye on it so the food item you added doesn't fly up and burn.

13. Reheating Leftovers

To warm your leftovers, it is suggested that you use an air fryer. Some foods, such as fried snacks or dishes coated in breadcrumbs, are supposed to get soggy when you heat them again. By doing it in a Ninja Air Fryer, you can make sure that your leftovers become as crispy as they were the day they were made. Air fryers have a remarkable ability to heat up and elevate leftovers. Just don't put liquid-based or heavily sauced dishes, including pasta and stew, in the air fryer, as it might create a mess and dry out the meal.

14. Holding Cheese Slices with a Toothpick

If you are preparing burgers in the air fryer and need to add a cheese slice to melt on top, place it with a toothpick so it doesn't fly away, as it is lightweight. You can save a piece of bread this way by placing it on a toothpick and pushing it through the bread and into one of the holes in the basket.

15. Prepare Healthy Veggie Chips

You can also use your Ninja Air Fryer to start from scratch and make your own vegetable chips. To do that, just cut zucchini or any other vegetable you like, such as pumpkin, and cover it with a mixture of flour, breadcrumbs, eggs, and parmesan. Then put it in a foil-lined air fryer for crisp, homemade veggie chips.

COOKING MEASUREMENT CONVERSION CHART

Dry Measurements	
Measurement	**Equivalent**
1 pound	16 ounces
1 cup	16 tablespoons
3/4 cup	12 tablespoons
2/3 cup	10 tablespoons plus 2 teaspoons
½ cup	8 tablespoons
3/8 cup	6 tablespoons
1/3 cup	5 tablespoons plus 1 teaspoon
¼ cup	4 tablespoons
1/6 cup	2 tablespoons plus 2 teaspoons
1/8 cup	2 tablespoons
1/16 cup	1 tablespoon
1 tablespoon	3 teaspoons
1/8 teaspoon	Pinch
1/16 teaspoon	Dash
½ cup butter	1 stick of butter

Liquid Measurements	
Measurement	**Equivalent (rounded for ease of use)**
4 quarts	1 gallon
2 quarts	½ gallon
1 quart	¼ gallon
2 pints	1 quart
4 cups	1 quart
2 cups	½ quart
2 cups	1 pint
1 cup	½ pint
1 cup	¼ quart
1 cup	8 fluid ounces
3/4 cup	6 fluid ounces
2/3 cup	5.3 fluid ounces
½ cup	4 fluid ounces
1/3 cup	2.7 fluid ounces
¼ cup	2 fluid ounces
1 tablespoon	0.5 fluid ounces

U.S. to Metric Conversions	
U.S. Measurement	**Metric Conversion (rounded for ease of use)**
Weight Measurements	
1 pound	454 grams
8 ounces	227 grams
4 ounces	113 grams
1 ounce	28 grams
Volume Measurements	
4 quarts	3.8 liters
4 cups (1 quart)	0.95 liters
2 cups	473 milliliters
1 cup	237 milliliters
3/4 cup	177 milliliters
2/3 cup	158 milliliters
½ cup	118 milliliters
1/3 cup	79 milliliters
¼ cup	59 milliliters
1/5 cup	47 milliliters
1 tablespoon	15 milliliters
1 teaspoon	5 milliliters
½ teaspoon	2.5 milliliters
1/5 teaspoon	1 milliliter
Fluid Measurements	
34 fluid ounces	1 liter
8 fluid ounces	237 milliliters
3.4 fluid ounces	100 milliliters
1 fluid ounce	30 milliliters

Metric to U.S. Conversions	
Metric Measurement (rounded for ease of use)	**U.S. Conversion**
Weight Measurements	
500 grams	1.10 pounds
100 grams	3.5 ounces
50 grams	1.8 ounces
1 gram	0.04 ounces
Volume Measurements	
1 liter	0.26 gallons
1 liter	1.06 quarts
1 liter	2.1 pints

1 liter	4.2 cups
500 milliliters	2.1 cups
237 milliliters	1 cup
177 milliliters	3/4 cup
158 milliliters	2/3 cup
118 milliliters	½ cup
100 milliliters	2/5 cup
79 milliliters	1/3 cup
59 milliliters	¼ cup
47 milliliters	1/5 cup
15 milliliters	1 tablespoon
5 milliliters	1 teaspoon
2.5 milliliters	½ teaspoon
1 milliliter	1/5 teaspoon
Fluid Measurements	
1 liter	34 fluid ounces
237 milliliters	8 fluid ounces
100 milliliters	3.4 fluid ounces
30 milliliters	1 fluid ounce

BREAKFAST

NINJA AIR FRYER BREAKFAST PIZZA WITH ENGLISH MUFFINS

Preparation Time: 5 minutes | Cooking Time: 5 minutes | Servings: 6

Ingredients:

- Eggs - 2
- Ground sausage, cooked - 455 grams (1 pound)
- Shredded Colby Jack Cheese - 60 grams (½ cup)
- English muffins - 3
- Olive oil spray
- Salt and pepper, to taste
- Fennel seeds (optional)

Instructions:

1. Make sure to cook both the sausage and eggs before starting.
2. Coat the air fryer basket with a light layer of olive oil cooking spray, which will help the English muffins to crisp up and not stick to the basket.
3. Split the English muffins, making six total halves.
4. Place the English muffin halves in the air fryer basket, making sure not to overcrowd the basket. You may need to cook the muffins in two separate batches, depending on the size of your air fryer.
5. Lightly spray the English muffins with another layer of olive oil cooking spray to help them crisp up.
6. Top the six English muffin halves with the cooked sausage and cooked eggs.
7. Next, sprinkle the shredded cheese on top of the muffins.
8. If desired, add a dash of fennel seeds over the eggs for extra flavour, and season with salt and black pepper to taste.
9. Set the air fryer to 180°C (355°F) and cook for 5 minutes or until the cheese is melted and the English muffins are lightly toasted.
10. Remove the breakfast pizza from the air fryer basket and transfer them to a plate.
11. Repeat the process with any remaining English muffin halves.
12. Serve the air fryer breakfast pizza hot, and enjoy!

Cooking Tip: You can add your favourite toppings such as diced tomatoes, sliced mushrooms, chopped onions and bell pepper.

Nutrition Value:

Calories: 429 | Fat: 32g | Saturates: 11g | Carbs: 15g | Sugars: 1g | Fibre: 2g | Protein: 20g | Salt: 0.89g

LOW-CARB BREAKFAST CASSEROLE IN NINJA AIR FRYER

Preparation Time: 10 minutes | Cooking Time: 15 minutes | Servings: 8

Ingredients:

- Ground sausage - 455 grams (1 pound)
- White onion, diced - 13 grams (¼ Cup)
- Green bell pepper, diced - 1
- Whole eggs - 8
- Shredded Colby Jack Cheese - 60 grams (½ cup)
- Fennel seed - 1 teaspoon
- Garlic salt - ½ teaspoon

Instructions:

1. If you are using the Ninja Foodi, turn on the sauté function and let it heat up. If you are using an air fryer, heat a skillet on the stove.
2. Add the ground sausage to the pot of the Ninja Foodi or the skillet, breaking it into small pieces with a wooden spoon until it's browned and fully cooked.
3. Once the sausage is cooked, add in the chopped onion and green bell pepper. Stir and cook until the veggies are soft and the sausage is thoroughly cooked.
4. Take the 8.75 inch pan or Air Fryer pan and spray it with non-stick cooking spray. Make sure to coat the bottom and sides of the pan evenly.
5. Transfer the cooked sausage mixture to the bottom of the prepared pan.
6. Sprinkle the shredded cheese evenly over the sausage mixture.
7. Whisk the eggs in a separate bowl and then pour them evenly over the cheese and sausage.
8. Sprinkle the fennel seed and garlic salt evenly over the eggs.
9. If you're using a Ninja Foodi, place the rack in the low position and then place the pan on top. If you're using an air fryer, put the dish directly into the basket.
10. Select the Air Crisp mode and cook for 15 minutes at 200°C (390°F).
11. If you are using an air fryer, set the air fryer timer to 15 minutes and temperature to 200°C (390°F).
12. Once the cooking time is up, carefully remove the pan from the air fryer.
13. Let the casserole cool down for a few minutes before slicing and serving. Enjoy your delicious and healthy air fryer breakfast casserole!

Nutrition Value:

Calories: 282 | Fat: 23g | Saturates: 8g | Carbs: 3g | Sugars: 2g | Fibre: 1g | Protein: 15g | Salt: 0.68g

AIR FRYER BREAKFAST DOUGHNUTS

Preparation Time: 30 minutes + rising | Cooking Time: 4 minutes | Servings: 12

Ingredients:

- Milk, lukewarm - 250 ml (1 cup)
- Active dry yeast or instant yeast - 2 ½ teaspoon
- Granulated sugar - 50 grams (¼ cup), plus 1 teaspoon
- Salt - ½ teaspoon
- Egg - 1
- Unsalted butter, melted - 4 tablespoons
- All-purpose flour - 360 grams (3 cups)
- Cooking oil spray

For the glaze:

- Unsalted butter - 6 tablespoons
- Powdered sugar - 240 grams (2 cups)
- Vanilla extract - 2 teaspoons
- Hot water - 4 tablespoons, or as needed

Instructions:

1. Mix the milk, one teaspoon of sugar, and yeast. Let it sit for 10 minutes until foamy.
2. Add the sugar, salt, egg, melted butter, and 2 cups of flour to the milk mixture. Mix on low speed, gradually adding the remaining cup of flour. Raise the speed to medium-low and knead until the dough is elastic and smooth.
3. Keep the dough covered in a greased bowl, and let it rise until doubled.
4. Roll out the dough on a floured surface to a thickness of approximately ½ inch. Cut out 10 to 12 doughnuts with a 3-inch cutter and remove the centre with a 1-inch cutter.
5. Transfer the doughnuts and holes to a floured parchment paper and cover with greased plastic wrap. Let them rise until they double in volume.
6. Preheat the air fryer to 180°C (360°F).
7. Grease the air fryer basket with oil spray, and then place the doughnuts in the basket.
8. Spray the doughnuts with oil spray and cook until golden brown, about 4 minutes.
9. Meanwhile, melt butter for the glaze in a saucepan. Stir in the powdered sugar and vanilla extract. Remove from heat and add hot water gradually until the icing is thin.
10. Dip the hot doughnuts and holes in the glaze. Keep them on a wire rack for some time to allow excess glaze to drip off. Serve and enjoy!

Nutrition Value:

1 Roll: Calories: 251 | Fat: 8g | Saturates: 5g | Carbs: 39g | Sugars: 15g | Fibre: 1g | Protein: 5g | Salt: 0.11g

BOURBON BACON
CINNAMON ROLLS IN AIR FRYER

Preparation Time: 25 minutes | Cooking Time: 10 minutes | Servings: 8

Ingredients:

- Bacon strips - 8
- Bourbon - 140 grams (¾ cups)
- Refrigerated cinnamon rolls with icing - 1 tube (350 grams)
- Chopped pecans - 65 grams (½ cup)
- Maple syrup - 2 tablespoons
- Minced fresh ginger root - 1 teaspoon

Instructions:

1. Place the bacon strips in a shallow dish and pour bourbon over it. Cover the dish and refrigerate it overnight.
2. Remove the bacon from the dish and pat them dry. Discard the bourbon.
3. Cook the bacon in batches over medium heat in a large skillet until almost crispy but still bendable. Place the bacon on paper towels to drain. Keep one teaspoon of bacon drippings.
4. Preheat the air fryer to 175°C (350°F).
5. Divide the dough into eight rolls, reserving the icing packet.
6. Unroll the spiral rolls into long strips and flatten the dough to make 6x1-inch strips.
7. Place a strip of bacon on each dough strip, trimming the bacon if necessary. Roll the dough into a spiral again and pinch the ends to seal. Repeat with the remaining dough.
8. Put four rolls on an ungreased tray in the air fryer basket and cook for 5 minutes. Flip the rolls over and cook until golden brown, about four more minutes.
9. While the rolls are cooking, mix the pecans and maple syrup in a bowl. In another bowl, combine the ginger with the contents of the icing packet.
10. Heat the remaining bacon drippings over medium heat in the same skillet. Add the pecan mixture and frequently stir until lightly toasted, which takes about 2 to 3 minutes.
11. Drizzle half the icing over the warm cinnamon rolls and top with half the pecans. Repeat to make a second batch.
12. Serve hot!

Cooking Tip: Air fryer cook times may vary depending on the brand, so it's recommended to begin checking at the first suggested time and adjust as needed.

Nutrition Value:

Calories: 267 | Fat: 14g | Saturates: 3g | Carbs: 28g | Sugars: 13g | Fibre: 1g | Protein: 5g | Salt: 0.49g

CROQUETTES WITH EGG AND ASPARAGUS IN AIR FRYER

Preparation Time: 25 minutes | Cooking Time: 10 minutes | Servings: 8

Ingredients:

- Butter - 3 tablespoons
- All-purpose flour - 3 tablespoons
- Milk - 175 ml (¾ cup)
- Hard-boiled large eggs, chopped - 6
- Chopped fresh asparagus - 60 grams (½ cup)
- Chopped green onions - 50 grams (½ cup)
- Shredded cheddar cheese - 40 grams (⅓ cup)
- Minced fresh tarragon - 1 tablespoon
- Salt - ¼ teaspoon
- Pepper - ¼ teaspoon
- Panko bread crumbs - 50 grams (⅓ cup)
- Large eggs, beaten - 3
- Cooking oil spray

Instructions:

1. Take a large saucepan, and melt the butter over medium heat on the stove. Stir in the flour until smooth and cook for 1 to 2 minutes until lightly browned.
2. Gradually whisk in the milk and continue to cook and stir until the mixture thickens.
3. Stir in the hard-boiled eggs, asparagus, green onions, cheese, tarragon, salt, and pepper. Gently mix everything together until well combined.
4. Refrigerate the mixture for at least 2 hours to allow it to firm up.
5. Preheat your air fryer to 175°C (350°F).
6. Shape the egg mixture into twelve 3-inch long ovals, using about ¼ cup of the mixture for each oval.
7. Place the bread crumbs and eggs in two different shallow bowls. Roll each oval in the bread crumbs, dip in the egg and roll in the bread crumbs again, patting to help the coating adhere.
8. Place the croquettes in a single layer on a greased tray in the air fryer basket.
9. Spritz the croquettes with cooking spray and cook until golden brown, which should take around 8 to 10 minutes.
10. Turn the croquettes over and spritz them with cooking spray. Cook for an additional 3 to 5 minutes or until they are golden brown on all sides.
11. Remove the croquettes from the air fryer and serve hot.

Nutrition Value:

2 Croquettes: Calories: 294 | Fat: 17g | Saturates: 8g | Carbs: 18g | Sugars: 3g | Fibre: 1g | Protein: 15g | Salt: 0.35g

NINJA AIR FRYER BREAKFAST BOMBS

Preparation Time: 35 minutes | Cooking Time: 15 minutes | Servings: 10

Ingredients:

- Bacon slices, cut into ½-inch pieces - 4
- Butter - 1 tablespoon
- Eggs, beaten - 2
- Pepper - ¼ teaspoon
- Grands Flaky! Biscuits - 1 can
- Sharp cheddar cheese, cut into ten 3/4-inch cubes - 60 grams (2 ounces)
- Egg - 1
- Water - 1 tablespoon

Instructions:

1. Cut two 8-inch rounds of cooking parchment paper. Place one circle in the bottom of the air fryer basket and spray it with cooking spray.
2. On a large skillet, sauté the bacon over medium heat until crisp. Transfer the bacon onto a paper towel. Wipe the skillet with a paper towel to absorb excess grease.
3. In the same skillet, melt butter on medium heat. Add 2 beaten eggs and pepper to the skillet. Cook until the eggs are thickened but still moist, stirring frequently. Remove the skillet from heat and stir in the bacon. Let it cool for 5 minutes.
4. While the bacon and eggs are cooling, you can prepare the biscuit dough. Pull apart the canned biscuit dough into 5 biscuits and then separate each biscuit into 2 layers. Press each layer into a 4-inch round.
5. Spoon 1 heaping tablespoonful of the bacon and egg mixture onto the centre of each round. Top the mixture with one cube of cheese. Gently fold the edges up over the filling, pinching them to seal.
6. Beat the remaining egg and water in a small bowl. Brush the biscuit bombs on all sides with the egg wash.
7. Place 5 biscuit bombs on the parchment paper in the air fryer basket, seam sides down. Spray both sides of the second parchment circle with cooking spray. Place it on top of the biscuit bombs in the basket. Then, add the remaining 5 biscuit bombs on top of the second parchment round.
8. Set the air fryer to 150°C (325°F) and cook the biscuit bombs for 8 minutes.
9. After 8 minutes, remove the top parchment round, flip the biscuits and place them in the basket in a single layer.
10. Cook them again for 4 to 6 minutes or until they reach an internal temperature of at least 75°C (165°F).
11. Once they're ready, remove them from the air fryer and enjoy!

Nutrition Value:

1 Biscuit Bomb: Calories: 160 | Fat: 9g | Saturates: 5g | Carbs: 14g | Sugars: 2g | Fibre: 0g | Protein: 5g | Salt: 0.36g

SOFT-BOILED SCOTCH EGGS IN AIR FRYER

Preparation Time: 28 minutes | Cooking Time: 12 minutes | Servings: 6

Ingredients:

- Large eggs - 6
- Ground breakfast sausage - 455 grams (1 pound)
- Wondra - 60 grams (¼ cup)
- Garlic powder - ½ teaspoon
- Egg, beaten - 1
- Panko crumbs - 150 grams (1 cup)
- Brown sugar - 1 tablespoon
- Chilli powder - ½ teaspoon

Instructions:

1. Fill a pan halfway with water and bring to a boil. Place the eggs into the boiling water, reduce the heat and cover the pan. Simmer for exactly 6 minutes.
2. After 6 minutes, immediately submerge the eggs in ice water for 10 minutes.
3. Next, roll the ground sausage into 6 equal balls and place them in the refrigerator.
4. Peel, rinse and pat the eggs dry. Set aside.
5. Remove the cold sausage balls from the fridge. Place a meatball in the centre of an 8x8 parchment square.
6. Gently pat the ball into a ¼-inch thick oval, roughly 3 eggs long and 2 eggs wide.
7. Take the parchment square in your palm and lay an egg on top of the oval.
8. Wrap the sausage around the egg. Ensure it's wrapped evenly and seal the edges.
9. Pass the egg from one hand to the other to smooth out the surface.
10. In one bowl, mix the Wondra and garlic powder, the beaten egg in another, and the Panko crumbs, brown sugar, and chilli powder in another.
11. Roll each sausage-covered egg in the flour mixture, dip in the beaten egg, and roll in the Panko crumbs.
12. Pass the eggs carefully from one hand to the other a couple of times to help form the outside crust a bit.
13. Place the breaded eggs on a plate until you have enough done for one batch (2-6, depending on the size of your air-fryer).
14. Preheat the air fryer to 190°C (380°F) for 10 minutes.
15. Set Scotch eggs on the air fryer basket, leaving space around each one.
16. Air-fry the eggs for 12 minutes, turning them halfway through for even browning.
17. Serve alone or with your favourite dipping sauce.

Nutrition Value:

1 Egg: Calories: 342 | Fat: 26g | Saturates: 9g | Carbs: 7g | Sugars: 2g | Fibre: 1g | Protein: 19g | Salt: 0.59g

AIR FRIED BRUSSELS SPROUTS HASH

Preparation Time: 10 minutes | Cooking Time: 16 minutes | Servings: 4

Ingredients:

- Brussels sprouts - 250 grams (2 cups)
- Small red onion - 1
- Baby red potatoes - 360 grams (2 cups)
- Avocado oil - 2 tablespoons
- Salt - ½ teaspoons
- Black pepper - ½ teaspoons
- Eggs - 4 (optional)
- Avocado - 1 (optional)

Instructions:

1. Place the potatoes in a medium-sized stockpot and cover them with salted water.
2. Bring the water to a boil. Lower the heat and simmer the potatoes until they are tender enough to be easily pierced with a fork, which should take around 15 minutes.
3. Drain the water from the pot and let the potatoes cool down. Then, slice them in halves.
4. Next, wash the brussels sprouts and shred or thinly slice them using a mandolin or sharp knife.
5. Slice the onion into ¼-inch slices.
6. Preheat the air fryer to 190°C (375°F).
7. Place a sheet of parchment paper on the air fryer basket and poke a few holes in it with a knife or fork.
8. Add the potatoes to the basket in an even layer. Spray or drizzle them with half of the oil and season lightly with salt and pepper.
9. Cook the potatoes for 10 minutes if you are using pre-boiled potatoes or 22-25 minutes if you are using raw potatoes. Turn the potatoes once halfway through the cooking time to ensure that they cook evenly on all sides.
10. Once the potatoes start to get crispy, add the brussels sprouts and onions to the basket. Spray or drizzle all the veggies with the remaining oil and cook for another 6 minutes, stirring or shaking once halfway through.
11. Season with more salt and pepper to taste.
12. If you want to serve a complete meal, add avocado and eggs or your protein of choice.
13. Enjoy your brussels sprouts potato hash for breakfast!

Nutrition Value:

1 Egg: Calories: 342 | Fat: 26g | Saturates: 9g | Carbs: 7g | Sugars: 2g | Fibre: 1g | Protein: 19g | Salt: 0.59g

NINJA AIR FRYER KETO MUFFINS

Preparation Time: 10 minutes | Cooking Time: 18 minutes | Servings: 4

Ingredients:

- Greek yoghourt - 70 grams (¼ cup)
- Large egg - 1
- Water - 2 tablespoons
- Swerve Sweetener - 3 tablespoons
- Orange zest - 2 teaspoons
- Vanilla extract - ¼ teaspoons
- Orange extract - ¼ teaspoon
- Almond flour - 70 grams (½ cup)
- Coconut flour - 2 tablespoons
- Unflavoured whey protein powder (or egg white powder) - 2 tablespoons
- Baking powder - ¾ teaspoons
- Salt - ⅛ teaspoons
- Fresh cranberries, chopped in half - 28 grams (¼ cup)

Instructions:

1. Take a medium-sized bowl and add yoghurt, egg, water, sweetener, orange zest, vanilla extract, and orange extract. Whisk them together until the ingredients are well combined.

2. Once the wet ingredients are well combined, add almond flour, coconut flour, whey protein, baking powder, and salt to the bowl. Mix everything until the dry ingredients are well incorporated into the wet mixture.

3. After mixing the dry ingredients into the wet mixture, add chopped cranberries to the bowl. Stir them in so that the cranberries are evenly distributed throughout the mixture.

4. Take four silicone muffin cups and divide the mixture equally among them. Use a spoon or spatula to level the mixture in each cup.

5. Preheat the air fryer to 155°C (310°F).

6. Once the air fryer is heated, place the muffin cups in the bottom of the air fryer. Make sure they are not touching each other or the sides of the air fryer.

7. Set the timer for 15 to 18 minutes. Bake the muffins until they turn golden brown, and the tops become firm to the touch.

8. Once the muffins are ready, remove them from the air fryer and let them cool in the cups for a few minutes.

9. Serve and enjoy your keto cranberry orange muffins! Muffins taste best the day they are made, but they can also be stored and enjoyed later.

Nutrition Value:

1 Muffin: Calories: 150 | Fat: 14g | Saturates: 6g | Carbs: 7g | Sugars: 1g | Fibre: 3g | Protein: 4g | Salt: 0.19g

AIR-FRIED MINI BANANA BREAD LOAF

Preparation Time: 5 minutes | Cooking Time: 30 minutes | Servings: 4

Ingredients:

- Banana small to medium, mashed - 1
- Large egg - 1
- Brown sugar - 2 tablespoons
- Olive oil - 2 tablespoons
- Milk - 60 ml (¼ cup)
- All-purpose flour - 95 grams (¾ cup)
- Baking soda - ½ teaspoon
- Salt - 1 pinch
- Vanilla - ½ teaspoon
- Cinnamon or nutmeg - 1 pinch (optional)
- Raspberries, blueberries, chocolate chips, coconut, nuts (optional)

Instructions:

1. Choose a small ovenproof baking pan, glass dish or mini loaf pan that fits comfortably into your air fryer. Line the chosen pan with baking paper and spray it with olive oil to prevent the cake from sticking.
2. Set the air fryer to preheat at 160°C (320°F).
3. In a small bowl, crack open the egg and whisk it together with the mashed banana until smooth. Next, add brown sugar, oil, and milk, and whisk the ingredients together until they are well combined.
4. Add all-purpose flour, baking soda, a pinch of cinnamon or nutmeg, vanilla, and salt to the wet mixture. Mix until all the ingredients are just combined. Fold in any desired mix-ins, such as raspberries, blueberries, chocolate chips, nuts or coconut, until evenly distributed in the batter.
5. Pour the batter into the prepared baking pan, and spread it evenly with a spatula.
6. Place the pan in the preheated air fryer and bake the cake for 25 to 35 minutes. Check if it is done by inserting a skewer or toothpick into the centre of the loaf. It should come out clean; however, a little bit of stickiness is okay. Depending on the kind of air fryer you have, baking time may vary, but it usually takes around 30 to 35 minutes.
7. Let the banana cake cool in the pan for about 10 minutes. Then, carefully remove the cake from the pan and transfer it to a wire rack to cool completely.
8. Once it is cool, slice and serve as desired!

Nutrition Value:

Calories: 233 | Fat: 9g | Saturates: 1g | Carbs: 34g | Sugars: 13g | Fibre: 1g | Protein: 5g | Salt: 0.17g

LUNCH

EASY NINJA AIR FRYER CHICKEN WINGS

Preparation Time: 10 minutes | Cooking Time: 20 minutes | Servings: 6

Ingredients:

- Chicken wings - 680 grams (1.5 pounds)
- Dry ranch dressing - 30 grams
- Olive oil - 2 tablespoons

Instructions:

1. To prepare the chicken wings, begin by placing them on a cutting board. Using a sharp chef's knife, carefully remove the wingtips, which you can throw away.
2. Next, separate the drumettes from the wingettes by cutting at the joint.
3. In a medium-sized mixing bowl, combine the dry ranch dressing and olive oil to make the sauce.
4. Add the chicken wingettes and drumettes to the bowl, and toss until the wings are coated fully.
5. Preheat the air fryer to 200°C (400°F).
6. Using tongs, place the chicken wings in a single layer on the air fry pan.
7. Bake for 10 minutes before using tongs to flip the wings over. Cook for an additional 10 minutes or until the internal temperature of the wings reaches 75°C (165°F).
8. Serve the chicken wings while they're still hot. You can pair them with your favourite dipping sauce or incorporate them into a salad or recipe of your choice. Bon appetit!

Cooking Tip:

- For perfectly crispy chicken wings, it is important to fry them for a total of 20 minutes. Cook for 10 minutes on one side, flip them over and cook for 10 more minutes on the other side.
- We used the Ninja fryer with excellent results, but any air fryer model will work.
- If you are cooking frozen chicken wings, increase the total cooking time to 25 minutes or until the internal temperature of the wings reaches 75°C (165°F).
- You can store the cooked wings in an air-tight container in the refrigerator for up to 3 days. To reheat them, return the wings to the air fryer for 10 minutes. While these wings can still be enjoyed as leftovers, they taste best served on the day they are fried.

Nutrition Value:

Calories: 190 | Fat: 14g | Saturates: 3g | Carbs: 3g | Sugars: 1g | Fibre: 1g | Protein: 11g | Salt: 0.4g

AIR FRYER STUFFED MUSHROOMS

Preparation Time: 5 minutes | Cooking Time: 7 minutes | Servings: 4

Ingredients:

- Mushrooms, with stems removed - 225 grams (8 ounces)
- Cream cheese - 113 grams (4 ounces)
- Turkey bacon - 4 strips
- Cheddar cheese shredded - 120 grams (1 cup)
- Salt - ½ teaspoon
- Garlic powder - ½ teaspoon
- Pepper - ¼ teaspoon

Instructions:

1. Clean the mushrooms by gently washing them with cold water. Pat them dry with a paper towel.
2. Remove the tops of the mushrooms from the stems and set aside.
3. In a medium bowl, mix the softened cream cheese, crumbled bacon, shredded cheddar cheese, salt, garlic powder, and pepper until well combined and the mixture has a creamy texture.
4. Spoon the cream cheese mixture into the mushroom caps, filling each one to the top.
5. Preheat your air fryer to 200°C (400°F).
6. Lightly spray or brush the air fryer basket with oil to prevent sticking.
7. Gently place the stuffed mushrooms into the air fryer basket, ensuring they are not stacked or overlapping.
8. Air fry the mushrooms for 5 to 7 minutes, or until the tops turn golden brown and the filling is hot and bubbly.
9. Use tongs or a spatula to remove the mushrooms from the air fryer basket.
10. Serve the stuffed mushrooms hot!

Cooking Tip: You can also sprinkle some additional shredded cheese on top of the mushrooms before air frying for an extra crispy and cheesy crust. To add more protein to your stuffed mushrooms, include chopped crab meat, cooked ground meat, and any cheese or sauces you want to mix in.

Nutrition Value:

Calories: 234 | Fat: 21g | Saturates: 3g | Carbs: 4g | Sugars: 1g | Fibre: 1g | Protein: 12g | Salt: 0.64g

FRIED RICE WITH SESAME-SRIRACHA SAUCE IN AIR FRYER

Preparation Time: 20 minutes | Cooking Time: 10 minutes | Servings: 2

Ingredients:

- Cooked white rice - 400 grams (2 cups)
- Vegetable oil - 1 tablespoon
- Toasted sesame oil - 2 teaspoons
- Kosher salt and ground black pepper, to taste
- Sriracha - 1 teaspoon
- Soy sauce - 1 teaspoon
- Sesame seeds - ½ teaspoon, plus more for topping
- Large egg, lightly beaten - 1
- Frozen peas and carrots, thawed - 175 grams (1 cup)

Instructions:

1. In a mixing bowl, combine 2 cups of cooked white rice with 1 tablespoon of vegetable oil, 1 teaspoon of toasted sesame oil, and 1 tablespoon of water. Add salt and pepper to the mixture and toss to ensure it is well seasoned.
2. Transfer the rice mixture to a round air fryer insert, metal cake pan, or foil pan.
3. Put the pan in the air fryer and cook at 175°C (350°F) for about 12 minutes, stirring halfway through, until the rice is lightly toasted and crunchy.
4. While the rice is cooking, stir together 1 teaspoon of sriracha, 1 teaspoon of soy sauce, ½ teaspoon of sesame seeds (preferably toasted), and 1 teaspoon of sesame oil in a small bowl.
5. Once the rice is toasted and crunchy, open the air fryer and pour 1 beaten egg over the rice. Close the air fryer and cook for about 4 minutes until the egg cooks.
6. Open the air fryer again, add 1 cup of thawed frozen peas and carrots, and stir into the rice to distribute and break up the egg. Close the air fryer and cook for 2 more minutes to heat the peas and carrots.
7. Once the fried rice is ready, spoon it into bowls, drizzle some sauce over it, and sprinkle with additional sesame seeds for added flavour and texture.
8. Enjoy!

Nutrition Value:

Calories: 263 | Fat: 9g | Saturates: 3g | Carbs: 39g | Sugars: 1g | Fibre: 2g | Protein: 7g | Salt: 0.24g

NINJA AIR FRYER TACO PIE

Preparation Time: 20 minutes | Cooking Time: 10 minutes | Servings: 2

Ingredients:

- Tortilla Shells - 6
- Refried beans - 1 can
- Ground beef - 455 grams (1 pound)
- Cheddar cheese -226 grams (2 cups)
- Taco Seasonings

Instructions:

1. Begin by spraying the bottom of a Fat Daddio or springform pan with cooking spray.
2. In a different non-stick pan, cook the ground beef over medium heat until it is browned, breaking up large chunks of meat with a wooden spoon or spatula.
3. Once the beef is cooked, add the taco seasoning and water according to the directions on the seasoning packet. Stir the mixture together and let it simmer for a few minutes until the sauce thickens and the flavours meld together.
4. Place a tortilla shell in the bottom of the prepared pan. Spread a light layer of refried beans on top of the tortilla.
5. Spoon a layer of taco meat on top of the beans. Spread it out evenly, covering the entire surface of the tortilla.
6. Sprinkle a layer of shredded cheese on top of the meat. Use as much or as little cheese as you prefer.
7. Repeat the layers of tortilla, beans, meat, and cheese until your pan is full. Depending on the size of your pan and the number of ingredients you use, you may have 3-5 layers.
8. Once you have added the final layer of cheese, place a tortilla shell on top of the cheese. This will help hold everything in place and create a crispy, crunchy top layer.
9. Transfer the pan to the bottom of your air fryer. Cook on air crisp at 200°C (400°F) for 5 minutes, or until the cheese is bubbly and the edges of the tortillas are crispy and golden brown.
10. Carefully remove the pan from the air fryer and let it cool for a few minutes before slicing and serving.

Nutrition Value:

Calories: 628 | Fat: 39g | Saturates: 17g | Carbs: 28g | Sugars: 1g | Fibre: 6g | Protein: 41g | Salt: 0.98g

CRISPY AIR-FRIED CAULIFLOWER GNOCCHI

Preparation Time: 20 minutes | Cooking Time: 10 minutes | Servings: 2

Ingredients:

- Cauliflower Gnocchi - 1 Bag
- Olive Oil - 2 tablespoons
- Salt and pepper, to taste
- Grated parmesan cheese, chopped herbs, marinara sauce (optional)

Instructions:

1. Preheat your air fryer to 200°C (400°F).
2. While the air fryer heats up, place the frozen cauliflower gnocchi in a mixing bowl and toss with 2 tablespoons of olive oil. Use your hands or a spoon to ensure the gnocchi is coated evenly with oil.
3. Once the air fryer is heated, place the gnocchi in the air fryer basket in a single layer. If your air fryer is small, you may need to cook the gnocchi in batches.
4. Cook the gnocchi for 8 to 10 minutes, shaking the basket or flipping the gnocchi halfway through to ensure even cooking. The gnocchi should be crispy and golden brown on the outside.
5. Once the gnocchi is cooked to your liking, use tongs or a spatula to transfer it to a serving dish.
6. Season the gnocchi with salt and pepper to taste. You can also sprinkle grated Parmesan cheese or chopped herbs over the top for added flavour.
7. Serve the gnocchi hot either on its own or with your favourite dipping sauce. Enjoy!

Nutrition Value:

Calories: 158 | Fat: 8g | Saturates: 1g | Carbs: 19g | Sugars: 3g | Fibre: 4g | Protein: 5g | Salt: 0.16g

AIR-FRIED MAC AND CHEESE BALLS

Preparation Time: 15 minutes | Cooking Time: 12 minutes | Servings: 16

Ingredients:

- Leftover mac and cheese - 600 grams (4 cups)
- Eggs, beaten - 2
- Seasoned bread crumbs - 300 grams (2 cups)

Instructions:

1. Chill leftover mac and cheese in the fridge for 3 hours.
2. Once the mac and cheese are chilled, scoop about 1 ½ tablespoons of mac and cheese, roll it, and form it into a ball. Repeat until you have about 16 balls.
3. Dip each ball in the beaten egg and then roll it in the bread crumbs, ensuring the entire ball gets coated in the bread crumbs.
4. Freeze the balls for 30 minutes while you preheat your air fryer to 180°C (360°F).
5. Once the air fryer is heated, carefully place the mac and cheese balls in, ensuring they don't touch each other. Depending on the size of your air fryer, this may need to be cooked in multiple batches.
6. Fry for 10 to 12 minutes until they turn golden brown.
7. Use tongs to carefully remove the mac and cheese balls from the air fryer and transfer them to a serving dish.
8. Serve hot, and enjoy your crispy air-fried mac and cheese balls!

Cooking Tip:

- Use a firmer mac and cheese because using leftover mac and cheese with a runny cheese sauce can cause the balls to become too soft and fall apart when air frying.
- Chill the mac and cheese for at least 3 hours or overnight so it can hold its shape better when forming into balls.
- Avoid letting the mac and cheese balls touch each other in the air fryer. Cook them in batches to give them enough room to cook evenly and prevent them from sticking together.

Nutrition Value:

Calories: 236 | Fat: 7g | Saturates: 1g | Carbs: 34g | Sugars: 1g | Fibre: 1g | Protein: 9g | Salt: 0.6g

CHINESE BBQ PORK IN AIR FRYER

Preparation Time: 10 minutes | Cooking Time: 15 minutes | Servings: 5

Ingredients:

- Pork belly or rashers - 1 kilogram

For marinade

- Five spice powder - 1 teaspoon
- Salt - 2.5 teaspoons
- Pepper, to taste
- White sugar - 4 tablespoons
- Soy sauce - 1 tablespoon
- Hoisin sauce - 2 tablespoons

- Chinese cooking wine - 1 tablespoon
- Honey - 2 tablespoons
- Garlic cloves, finely chopped - 2
- Red fermented tofu, mashed - 2 cubes (20 grams)
- Red fermented tofu, liquid - 3 teaspoons

For baste

- Honey - 3 tablespoons
- Marinade - 3 tablespoons

- Water - 1 teaspoon

Instructions:

1. In a bowl, combine the marinade ingredients. Set aside 3 tablespoons of marinade in a small container and store it in the fridge. This will be used as the baste later on.
2. Cut the pork into pieces that will fit into your air fryer. The pork should be cut to a thickness of 2 cm. Remove the pork rinds and save it for another recipe.
3. Place the pork and marinade in a zip-lock bag and shake it until the pork is coated fully. Marinate the pork for 1 to 2 days in the fridge.
4. When ready to cook, remove the pork from the fridge and let it sit for 30 minutes.
5. Preheat the air fryer to 200°C (400°F).
6. Combine the 3 tablespoons of the stored marinade with other baste ingredients.
7. Spray the air fryer basket with oil and place the pork on top.
8. Use a brush to baste the pork on both sides with the prepared baste.
9. Cook the pork for 6 minutes in the air fryer at 200°C (400°F).
10. Remove the pork from the air fryer, baste it again on both sides, and cook for another 6 minutes on the side that was previously facing down.
11. Flip the pork one more time and cook for roughly 2-3 minutes or until the pork is cooked and there is a decent amount of char at the edges. You may need to repeat the cooking, flipping, basting process a few more times to achieve the desired look.

Nutrition Value:

Calories: 1175 | Fat: 106g | Saturates: 39g | Carbs: 34g | Sugars: 31g | Fibre: 1g | Protein: 20g | Salt: 1.7g

NINJA AIR FRYER EGG ROLLS

Preparation Time: 15 minutes | Cooking Time: 12 minutes | Servings: 8

Ingredients:

- Egg roll wrappers (homemade or store-bought) - 8
- Cole slaw bagged with carrots - 180 grams (2 cups)
- Carrots, shredded - 40 grams (½ cup)
- Green onions - 10 grams (¼ cup)
- Soy sauce - 2 tablespoons
- Ginger paste - 1 teaspoon
- Olive oil - 2 tablespoons
- Rice noodles, prepared - 100 grams (3.5 oz)
- Olive oil spray

Instructions:

1. Fill a large pot with 4 quarts of water and place it over high heat. Bring the water to a boil.
2. Add the packaged rice noodles to the boiling water and use a utensil to stir them, separating them from one another. Allow the noodles to cook until they are barely tender. This should take approximately 2 to 3 minutes.
3. Drain the noodles and keep them in a bowl.
4. Add cabbage, carrots, onions, and soy sauce to the bowl of noodles. Mix the ingredients well.
5. Over medium heat on the stovetop, cook the cabbage mix. Add the ginger paste to the mixture and continue cooking. Toss everything together to combine the flavours.
6. If desired, add pre-cooked diced chicken to the cabbage mix and stir everything together.
7. Lay an egg roll wrapper on a clean, flat work surface.
8. Spoon some of the coleslaw mixture into the centre of the wrapper.
9. Brush the outer edges of the wrapper with water to help it stick together. Fold the sides of the wrapper inwards like an envelope and then roll it up tightly. Add a swipe of water to the end of the wrapper if needed to ensure it stays closed.
10. Spray the egg rolls with olive oil and put them into the air fryer basket.
11. Set the air fryer to 190°C (375°F) and cook the egg rolls for 5 to 8 minutes, flipping them halfway, until they are crispy on the outside.
12. Serve the egg rolls hot!

Nutrition Value:

Calories: 134 | Fat: 4g | Saturates: 1g | Carbs: 22g | Sugars: 1g | Fibre: 1g | Protein: 3g | Salt: 0.36g

NINJA AIR FRYER TENDER PRIME RIB

Preparation Time: 5 minutes | Cooking Time: 1 hour 15 minutes | Servings: 5-6

Ingredients:

- Prime Rib - 3 kilograms (6 pounds)
- Olive oil - 3 tablespoons
- Salt - 1 ½ teaspoons
- Black pepper - 1 ½ teaspoons
- Smoked paprika - 1 teaspoon
- Garlic powder - 1 teaspoon
- Minced garlic - about 10 cloves
- Freshly chopped or dried rosemary - ½ teaspoon
- Freshly chopped or dried thyme - ½ teaspoon

Instructions:

1. Preheat the air fryer to 200°C (400°F).
2. Rub the prime rib generously with olive oil, ensuring that every part of the meat is coated entirely to help seal in moisture and flavour.
3. Sprinkle salt, black pepper, paprika, and garlic powder over the prime rib, covering it evenly.
4. Sprinkle crushed garlic, rosemary and thyme over the prime rib. Fresh herbs are best, but dried herbs work as well.
5. Gently place the seasoned prime rib in the air fryer basket, making sure it's positioned properly to ensure even cooking.
6. Cook the prime rib in the air fryer at 200°C (400°F) for 20 minutes.
7. After 20 minutes, lower the temperature to 315°C (160°F) and continue cooking for about 55 additional minutes, or until the internal temperature of the prime rib reaches 55°C (130°F) for medium-rare.
8. Check the temperature of the prime rib with an instant-read thermometer. If the temperature reading is still too low, let the rib cook for another 5 to 10 minutes.
9. Once the prime rib reaches the desired doneness take it out from the air fryer and let it rest for 20 to 30 minutes, allowing the meat to absorb its juices.
10. Finally, slice the prime rib and serve it with your favourite sides!

Cooking Tip: If the thermometer reading is lower than the desired temperature, continue cooking the prime rib in the air fryer for 5 to 10 more minutes, then check the temperature again.

Nutrition Value:

Calories: 810 | Fat: 65g | Saturates: 25g | Carbs: 1g | Sugars: 0g | Fibre: 0g | Protein: 51g | Salt: 0.41g

CORN ON THE COB IN AIR FRYER

Preparation Time: 5 minutes | Cooking Time: 13 minutes | Servings: 2

Ingredients:

- Corn - 2 ears
- Butter - 2 tablespoons
- Dried parsley - ½ teaspoon
- Sea salt - ¼ teaspoon
- Parmesan cheese (optional)

Instructions:

1. Preheat your air fryer to 200°C (400°F).
2. Take both ears of corn and shuck them carefully, removing any silk that may be left behind. If desired, cut the corn cobs in half for easier handling.
3. Mix melted butter, chopped parsley, and sea salt in a small bowl. Use a pastry brush to baste the butter mixture evenly onto the surface of the corn. For extra flavour, you can sprinkle some grated Parmesan cheese on top of the corn.
4. You can wrap the corn in aluminium foil to prevent it from drying out while cooking. Place the corn on a sheet of foil, brush with butter mixture, and wrap the foil around the corn, leaving enough space for air circulation.
5. Place the prepared corn inside the air fryer basket, side by side, leaving some space between them.
6. Close the basket and set the air fryer to cook for 12 to 14 minutes.
7. Check the corn occasionally and turn the cobs over halfway through to cook evenly. If you notice that some pieces of corn start to brown, it is a sign that they are ready to be removed from the air fryer.
8. Once the corn is cooked to your liking, take it out from the air fryer basket and transfer it to a serving plate.
9. Enjoy your air fryer corn on the cob!

How to Reheat Corn in the Air Fryer:

To reheat the corn, preheat the air fryer to 175°C (350°F), place the corn inside, and cook for 3-4 minutes until it is hot. Add more butter and salt to taste if needed.

How to Cook Frozen Corn on the Cob in the Air Fryer:

To cook frozen corn, preheat your air fryer to 190°C (380°F). Cook for 3 to 4 minutes, baste with the butter mixture and cook for another 10-12 minutes.

Nutrition Value:

Calories: 199 | Fat: 14g | Saturates: 8g | Carbs: 17g | Sugars: 4g | Fibre: 2g | Protein: 5g | Salt: 0.44g

APPETISERS

AIR-FRIED TOFU NUGGETS

Preparation Time: 10 minutes | Cooking Time: 15 minutes | Servings: 4

Ingredients:

- Extra firm tofu - 395 grams (14 oz)

For paste

- Nutritional yeast - 25 grams (⅓ cup)
- Soy sauce - 2 tablespoons
- Water - 60 ml (¼ cup)
- Garlic powder - 1 tablespoon

- Onion powder - 1 teaspoon
- Sweet paprika - 1 teaspoon
- Poultry spice or veggie broth powder - 1 teaspoon

Instructions:

1. If using the frozen tofu, you should fully thaw it out before starting. You can do this by transferring it to the refrigerator the day before you make it.
2. Squeeze the tofu for 10 to 30 minutes, depending on its firmness. This will help remove any excess water so it can absorb the flavours of the paste.
3. Prepare the air fryer by preheating it to 200°C (400°F).
4. In a large mixing bowl, combine all of the paste ingredients and stir to combine. If the mixture is too thin, add more nutritional yeast. If the mixture is too thick, add water in small measures.
5. Break the tofu into bite-sized chunks over the bowl, using your thumb to create craggy, rounded edges. This will help the tofu hold the paste better and take on a more nugget-like shape.
6. Lightly fold the chunks into the paste, careful not to break the tofu too much. Check to see that the tofu is coated evenly with the paste.
7. Use a pair of tongs to place the tofu into the basket of the air-fryer. Keep the tofu in a single layer along the bottom of the basket for best results. Be careful not to add excess paste to the basket, as it may result in burning.
8. Cook the tofu for 12 to 15 minutes, stopping halfway to shake the basket.
9. Serve the tofu right away!

Cooking Tip:

- Do not use silken tofu for this recipe.
- To reduce sodium content, you can use light soy sauce or mix the soy sauce with water by halving the soy sauce amount.

Nutrition Value:

Calories: 83 | Fat: 2g | Saturates: 1g | Carbs: 6g | Sugars: 1g | Fibre: 2g | Protein: 11g | Salt: 0.57g

AIR FRYER BACON WRAP
STUFFED JALAPENOS

Preparation Time: 10 minutes | Cooking Time: 14 minutes | Servings: 6

Ingredients:

- Jalapenos - 12
- Cream cheese - 230 grams (8 ounces)
- Shredded cheddar cheese - 60 grams (½ cup)
- Garlic powder - ¼ teaspoon
- Onion powder - ⅛ teaspoon
- Bacon slices, thinly cut - 12
- Salt and pepper, to taste

Instructions:

1. Cut the jalapenos in half lengthwise. Remove the stems and seeds, and scrape out the white membrane with a spoon. The more membrane you leave, the spicier the jalapenos will be.
2. In a bowl, combine the cream cheese, shredded cheddar cheese, garlic powder, onion powder, salt, and pepper. Mix the ingredients until they are well-combined.
3. Use a small spoon to scoop the cream cheese mixture into each jalapeno half, filling it just to the top.
4. Preheat the air fryer to 175°C (350°F) for about 3 minutes.
5. Cut each slice of bacon so you have two shorter pieces.
6. Take each jalapeno half and wrap it in one piece of bacon. Use toothpicks to secure the bacon to the jalapeno, if necessary.
7. Place the bacon-wrapped jalapenos in the air fryer basket in a single layer, making sure they do not overlap.
8. Air fry at 175°C (350°F) for 14 to 16 minutes or until the bacon is thoroughly cooked and crispy.
9. Remove the bacon-wrapped jalapenos from the air fryer basket with tongs and let them cool for a few minutes.
10. Enjoy your bacon-wrapped jalapenos!

Cooking Tip: You can refrigerate the jalapenos for up to 3 days. If reheating, use the air fryer or an oven to warm them up.

Nutrition Value:

Calories: 188 | Fat: 17g | Saturates: 10g | Carbs: 4g | Sugars: 3g | Fibre: 1g | Protein: 5g | Salt: 0.26g

CRISPY AIR-FRIED CHEESE CURDS

Preparation Time: 15 minutes | Cooking Time: 30 minutes | Servings: 5

Ingredients:

- Cheese curds - 450 grams (16 ounces)
- Bread crumbs - 295 grams (2 cups)
- Italian seasoning - 2 teaspoons
- Salt - ½ teaspoon
- Pepper - ¼ teaspoon
- Large eggs - 3
- Water - 1 tablespoon
- All purpose flour - 34 grams (¼ cup)

Instructions:

1. To prepare the breading mixture, take a wide, shallow bowl and combine bread crumbs, Italian seasoning, salt, and pepper. Use a whisk to mix all the ingredients.
2. In a separate bowl, add eggs and water, whisking until they are thoroughly combined.
3. Add the cheese curds and flour in a third bowl and toss them to coat evenly.
4. Next, dip the flour-coated cheese curds into the egg mixture, ensuring they are entirely covered. Now roll the egg-coated cheese curds in the breading mixture.
5. Repeat the dipping process by dipping the cheese curds back into the egg mixture and then coating them again with the breading mixture.
6. Preheat the air fryer to 200°C (400°F).
7. Place half of the breaded cheese curds in a single layer on the bottom of the basket. Spray the tops with cooking spray.
8. Cook the cheese curds in the air fryer at 200°C (400°F) for 5 to 6 minutes until they heat to the inside and have a crispy texture.
9. Repeat the air-frying process with the remaining cheese curds.
10. Once all the cheese curds are air fried, serve them with marinara sauce. Enjoy!

Cooking Tip: To reheat the cheese curds, preheat your air fryer to 190°C (380°F), place the curds in a single layer in the basket, and air fry for 3 to 5 minutes until they are hot all the way through.

Nutrition Value:

Calories: 604 | Fat: 35g | Saturates: 19g | Carbs: 39g | Sugars: 3g | Fibre: 2g | Protein: 31g | Salt: 0.26g

HOMEMADE AIR FRYER ONION RINGS

Preparation Time: 10 minutes | Cooking Time: 10 minutes | Servings: 4-6

Ingredients:

- Large Vidalia onion - 1
- Large eggs - 2
- Buttermilk - 160 ml (⅔ cup)
- All-purpose flour - 250 grams (⅔ cup)
- Kosher salt - ½ teaspoon
- Black pepper - ½ teaspoon
- Garlic powder - ½ teaspoon
- Panko bread crumbs - 225 grams (1 ½ cups)

Instructions:

1. Peel the large Vidalia onion and cut it into ½-inch thick slices. Separate the slices and place them on a plate. Set aside.
2. Take a wide, shallow bowl and lightly beat the eggs with the buttermilk until well combined.
3. Combine the flour, salt, pepper, and garlic powder in a second bowl.
4. Place the panko bread crumbs in a third mixing bowl.
5. Dredge each onion ring into the flour mixture, coating it entirely.
6. Next, dip the onion ring into the egg and buttermilk mixture, and then dredge it through the bread crumbs, pressing gently to adhere. Set aside on a baking sheet and repeat with the remaining onion rings. Spray them with an oil sprayer.
7. Preheat the air fryer to 190°C (380°F).
8. Transfer the onion rings into the air fryer basket in a single layer, nesting the smaller ones inside the larger ones but leaving a little space between each ring. Do not overcrowd the basket, and work in batches if necessary.
9. Air fry the onion rings for 9 to 12 minutes or until golden brown and crispy.
10. Once the onion rings are ready, remove them from the air fryer.
11. Sprinkle with salt if desired and serve immediately!

Cooking Tip: To reheat onion rings in the air fryer, preheat the appliance to 175°C (350°F) and place the leftover onion rings inside. Cook for 2 to 3 minutes until they are thoroughly warmed and crispy.

Nutrition Value:

Calories: 290 | Fat: 5g | Saturates: 2g | Carbs: 48g | Sugars: 5g | Fibre: 3g | Protein: 12g | Salt: 0.57g

CRAB RANGOON IN AIR FRYER

Preparation Time: 10 minutes | Cooking Time: 10 minutes | Servings: 4-6

Ingredients:

- Cream cheese - 140 grams (5 ounces)
- Crab meat - 140 grams (5 ounces)
- Green onions, chopped - 2
- Worcestershire -1 teaspoon
- Minced garlic - 1 ½ teaspoons
- Salt and pepper, to taste
- Olive oil cooking spray
- Wonton wrappers - 28
- Water

Instructions:

1. Combine softened cream cheese, canned crab meat, finely chopped green onions, Worcestershire sauce, minced garlic, salt and pepper. Mix everything well.
2. Place a wonton wrapper on a clean, dry cutting board.
3. Dip a pastry brush in water and use it to brush the edges of the wrapper.
4. Spoon 1 ½ teaspoons of the crab mixture onto the centre of the wrapper.
5. Fold two opposite corners of the wrapper to meet in the middle and form a triangle. Then fold the other corners to the centre and press down to seal the seams together.
6. Continue with the process until all the wonton wrappers are stuffed.
7. Preheat the air fryer to 180°C (360°F).
8. Lightly spritz the base of the air fryer basket with cooking spray.
9. Place the filled Crab Rangoons into the basket, leaving some space between each one.
10. Spritz the tops of the Crab Rangoons with a little more cooking spray.
11. Air fry the Crab Rangoons for 10 minutes, checking at the 5-minute mark and then every 2 minutes after, to check how brown and crispy you want them.
12. Once the Crab Rangoons are ready, remove them from the air fryer and let them cool for a few minutes before serving.
13. Serve the Crab Rangoons with sweet chilli sauce on the side for dipping.

Nutrition Value:

Calories: 201 | Fat: 10g | Saturates: 4g | Carbs: 20g | Sugars: 1g | Fibre: 1g | Protein: 8g | Salt: 0.38g

POTATO SKINS IN AIR FRYER

Preparation Time: 5 minutes | Cooking Time: 8 minutes | Servings: 8

Ingredients:

- Large cooked russet potatoes, cut in half - 4
- Olive oil - 1 tablespoon
- Salt and pepper, to taste
- Dressing seasoning, to taste (optional)
- Freshly grated cheddar cheese - 56 grams (½ cup)
- Cooked bacon, chopped - 2 slices
- Sour cream for topping (optional)
- Chopped green onions for topping (optional)

Instructions:

1. Take a spoon and scoop out a bit of the potato flesh from each halved cooked potato, forming a pocket. Be careful not to scoop out too much if you want to eat the potato flesh too. Set aside the scooped potato flesh.
2. Drizzle 1 tablespoon of olive oil over the top/flesh of the potato skins, and then use a brush to coat the entire potatoes with the oil.
3. Sprinkle a dash of salt and pepper over the potato skins.
4. If desired, sprinkle ranch dressing seasoning over the potato skins for added flavour.
5. Preheat the air fryer to 200°C (400°F).
6. Add the potato skins to the air fryer basket, skin side down.
7. Set the air fryer timer for 5 minutes.
8. Once the set time elapses, carefully remove the air fryer basket from the air fryer.
9. Stuff the potato skins with shredded cheese and bacon crumbles.
10. Close the air fryer basket and reduce the temperature to 175°C (350°F)
11. Set the timer for 2 minutes, and if necessary, you can add an extra minute to ensure the cheese is bubbly and melted nicely.
12. Carefully remove the potato skins from the air fryer basket using tongs or a spatula.
13. Top the potato skins with desired toppings like sour cream and chopped green onions.
14. Serve immediately and enjoy!

Nutrition Value:

Calories: 228 | Fat: 12g | Saturates: 5g | Carbs: 21g | Sugars: 1g | Fibre: 2g | Protein: 10g | Salt: 0.39g

GOLDEN AIR-FRIED FALAFELS

Preparation Time: 10 minutes | Cooking Time: 15 minutes | Servings: 4

Ingredients:

- Dried chickpeas, soaked overnight - 250 grams (1 cup)
- Garlic cloves, minced - 2
- Medium red onion, chopped - 1
- Fresh cilantro leaves (coriander) - 1 handful
- Ground coriander - 1 teaspoon
- Olive oil - 2 tablespoons
- Ground cumin - ¾ teaspoon
- Allspice - ¼ teaspoon
- Salt - ¾ teaspoon
- Baking powder - ½ teaspoon
- Almond flour ground almonds - 3 tablespoon

For the tahini yoghurt sauce:

- Yoghurt - 250 grams (1 cup)
- Lemon - 1
- Olive oil - 1 tablespoon
- Tahini paste - 1 teaspoon

Instructions:

1. Add chickpeas, garlic, onion, and cilantro leaves to a food processor and pulse until the mixture is coarsely ground.
2. Stream in olive oil while pulsing until the mixture is finely chopped but not mushy.
3. Transfer the mixture to a bowl and add all the spices, salt, baking powder, and ground almonds. Mix well.
4. Adjust seasoning to taste, then refrigerate the mixture for 1 hour.
5. Wet your hands and roll about 2 tablespoons of the falafel mixture into a small ball. Transfer the falafel ball to a plate or baking tray. Repeat with the remaining mixture until all falafel balls are formed.
6. Place the falafel in the air fryer basket, ensuring they do not touch.
7. Cook the falafel at 187°C (370°F) for 10 to 15 minutes, shaking the air fryer basket halfway through the cooking time. The falafel is ready when it's crisp and golden brown.
8. To prepare the tahini yoghurt sauce, mix all of its ingredients in a bowl.
9. Serve the air fryer falafels with the tahini yoghurt sauce, and enjoy!

Nutrition Value:

Calories: 366 | Fat: 18g | Saturates: 3g | Carbs: 40g | Sugars: 11g | Fibre: 10g | Protein: 15g | Salt: 0.5g

AIR FRYER THAI CHICKEN MEATBALLS

Preparation Time: 10 minutes | Cooking Time: 10 minutes | Servings: 12

Ingredients:

- Sweet chilli sauce - 120 ml (½ cup)
- Lime juice - 2 tablespoons
- Ketchup - 2 tablespoons
- Soy sauce - 1 teaspoon
- Large egg, lightly beaten - 1
- Panko bread crumbs - 90 grams (¾ cup)
- Green onion, finely chopped - 1
- Minced fresh cilantro - 1 tablespoon
- Salt - ½ teaspoon
- Garlic powder - ½ teaspoon
- Lean ground chicken - 455 grams (1 pound)

Instructions:

1. Preheat your air fryer to 175°C (350°F).
2. In a small bowl, combine chilli sauce, lime juice, ketchup, and soy sauce. Set aside ½ cup of the mixture for serving later. Feel free to modify the ingredient proportions according to your preference.
3. In a large bowl, beat the egg and then add the breadcrumbs, green onion, cilantro, salt, garlic powder, and the remaining 4 tablespoons of chilli sauce mixture. Mix everything lightly but thoroughly.
4. Add the ground chicken to the mixture in the large bowl and mix until well combined.
5. Shape the mixture into 12 balls of equal size, passing them from one hand to the other to smooth out the surface. You can wet your hands with water to help prevent the mixture from sticking.
6. Arrange the meatballs in a single layer on a greased tray in the air fryer basket. Cook until lightly browned, which takes approximately 4 to 5 minutes.
7. Flip the meatballs and cook for an additional 4 to 5 minutes, or until they are lightly browned and cooked through. If the meatballs are not cooked through, you can continue cooking them for a few more minutes until they reach an internal temperature of 75°C (165°F).
8. Serve the cooked meatballs with the reserved sauce and sprinkle with additional cilantro for extra flavour and garnish.
9. Enjoy your delicious air-fried chicken meatballs!

Nutrition Value:

Calories: 98 | Fat: 3g | Saturates: 1g | Carbs: 9g | Sugars: 6g | Fibre: 0g | Protein: 9g | Salt: 0.37g

AIR-FRIED SPICY BEEF SKEWERS

Preparation Time: 10 minutes | Cooking Time: 10 minutes | Servings: 12

Ingredients:

- Beef flank steak - 1 (450 grams)
- Rice vinegar - 250 ml (1 cup)
- Soy sauce - 250 ml (1 cup)
- Packed brown sugar - 50 grams (¼ cup)
- Fresh ginger root, minced - 2 tablespoons
- Garlic cloves, minced - 6
- Sesame oil - 3 teaspoons
- Sriracha chilli sauce - 2 teaspoons (or 1 teaspoon hot pepper sauce)
- Cornstarch - ½ teaspoon
- Sesame seeds (optional)
- Green onions, thinly sliced (optional)

Instructions:

1. Cut the beef flank steak into ¼-inch thick strips.
2. In a large bowl, whisk the next seven ingredients until blended.
3. Pour 1 cup of the marinade into a shallow dish.
4. Add the beef strips to the shallow dish with the marinade and turn to coat.
5. Cover the dish with plastic wrap and refrigerate the beef for 2 to 8 hours. Cover and refrigerate the remaining marinade as well.
6. Preheat the air fryer to 200°C (400°F).
7. Drain the beef, discarding the marinade in the dish.
8. Thread the beef onto 12 metal or soaked wooden skewers that fit into the air fryer. If your air fryer is smaller, you might need to work in batches; arrange the skewers in a single layer on a greased tray in the air fryer basket.
9. Cook until the meat reaches the desired doneness (for medium-rare, a thermometer should read 55°C (135°F); for medium, 60°C (140°F); for medium-well, 65°C (145°F), turning occasionally and frequently basting with ½ cup of the reserved marinade, for 4 to 5 minutes.
10. Meanwhile, to make the glaze, add the remaining marinade (about ¾ cup) to a boil in a small saucepan.
11. Whisk in ½ teaspoon of cornstarch and constantly whisk until thickened for 1 to 2 minutes.
12. Brush the skewers with the glaze just before serving. If you want, garnish with sesame seeds and thinly sliced green onions.

Nutrition Value:

2 kabobs: Calories: 264 | Fat: 10g | Saturates: 4g | Carbs: 18g | Sugars: 15g | Fibre: 0g | Protein: 24g | Salt: 1.48g

CRISPY AIR-FRIED BITE SIZE RAVIOLI

Preparation Time: 10 minutes | Cooking Time: 7 minutes | Servings: 12

Ingredients:

- Eggs - 2
- Panko bread crumbs - 120 grams (2 cups)
- Parmesan cheese, grated - 55 grams (½ cup)
- Salt - 1 teaspoon
- Garlic powder - 2 teaspoons
- Frozen mini cheese ravioli - 1 bag
- Oil spray

Instructions:

1. Take a bowl and crack in the eggs. Use a fork to whisk them thoroughly until they are well mixed.
2. Add the bread crumbs, grated parmesan cheese, garlic powder and salt in another bowl. Mix the ingredients well until they are combined.
3. Take a frozen ravioli out of the bag and dip it into the beaten egg, coating it completely.
4. Next, dip the ravioli into the bowl with the bread crumb mixture, pressing gently to help the coating stick.
5. Place the coated ravioli onto a cutting board and continue dipping the rest of the ravioli until you have enough to fill the basket.
6. Preheat the air fryer to 200°C (400°F) for 3 minutes.
7. Once the air fryer is heated, add the ravioli to the basket in a single layer. Make sure not to overcrowd or stack them.
8. Spray the ravioli with oil using a spray bottle.
9. Cook the ravioli in the air fryer at 200°C (400°F) for 7 minutes. After 3 to 4 minutes, you can take out the basket, flip the ravioli over, and spray them with more oil. This step is optional, but will make the ravioli a bit crispier.
10. If you want to cook the rest of the bag, repeat the steps above to make another batch.
11. Once the ravioli are ready, serve them with marinara or your favourite dipping sauce. You can also sprinkle fresh herbs and more Parmesan cheese on top for added flavour. Enjoy!

Cooking Tip: Add basil or Italian seasoning to the breadcrumbs for extra flavour, or use pre-seasoned breadcrumbs.

Nutrition Value:

Calories: 104 | Fat: 3g | Saturates: 1g | Carbs: 14g | Sugars: 1g | Fibre: 1g | Protein: 5g | Salt: 0.4g

DINNER

PINEAPPLE CHICKEN IN NINJA AIR FRYER

Preparation Time: 5 minutes | Cooking Time: 10 minutes | Servings: 2

Ingredients:

For the grilled chicken:

- Raw chicken breasts - 2
- Butter - 1 tablespoon
- Salt - ¼ teaspoon
- Pepper - ⅛ teaspoon

For the pineapple sauce:

- Pineapple juice - 120 ml (½ cup)
- brown sugar - 55 grams (¼ cup)
- Low-sodium soy sauce - 60 ml (¼ cup)
- Clove garlic, minced - 1 teaspoon
- Ground ginger - ⅛ teaspoon
- Cornstarch - 2 teaspoons
- Water - 2 teaspoons
- Chunks of fresh or canned pineapple (optional)

Instructions:

1. Preheat the air fryer to 190°C (380°F).
2. Mix together melted butter, salt, and pepper in a small bowl.
3. Dip the chicken breasts in the butter mixture and coat both sides well.
4. Place the chicken breasts in the air fryer basket and cook for 10 to 15 minutes.
5. You can use a meat thermometer to ensure that the chicken has reached the appropriate internal temperature. The internal temperature of the chicken needs to reach 75°C (165°F).
6. Once done, let the chicken rest for at least 5 minutes before slicing.
7. Meanwhile, prepare the pineapple sauce by combining pineapple juice, brown sugar, soy sauce, minced garlic, and ginger in a pan. Heat the mixture on medium heat and let it simmer for 5 minutes.
8. In a separate bowl, mix cornstarch and water to create a slurry. Add the slurry to the pineapple mixture and stir well. Let it simmer for one more minute while stirring.
9. Remove the sauce from the heat once it thickens and acquires a glossy texture.
10. Slice the rested chicken breasts into long strips.
11. Pour the pineapple sauce over the sliced chicken breasts, coating them entirely, or serve the sauce on the side.
12. If desired, add chunks of canned or fresh pineapple to the dish.

Nutrition Value:

Calories: 503 | Fat: 11g | Saturates: 5g | Carbs: 55g | Sugars: 47g | Fibre: 1g | Protein: 46g | Salt: 1.55g

AIR FRYER CHICKEN SHAWARMA BOWL

Preparation Time: 15 minutes | Cooking Time: 15 minutes | Servings: 4

Ingredients:

For the shawarma:

- Boneless skinless chicken thighs, cut into bite-size chunks - 455 grams (1 pound)
- Vegetable oil - 2 tablespoons
- Oregano - 2 teaspoons
- Cinnamon - 1 teaspoon
- Cumin - 1 teaspoon
- Coriander - 1 teaspoon
- Kosher salt - 1 teaspoon
- Allspice - ½ teaspoon

For the bowl:

- Cherry tomatoes, halved - 200 grams (1.5 cup)
- Cauliflower rice, cooked - 110 grams (1 cup)
- Small English cucumber, sliced - 1
- Salad greens -30 grams (2 cups)
- Pitted olives - 180 grams (1 cup)

For the dressing:

- Nonfat Greek yoghourt - 280 grams (1 cup)
- Lemon juice - 2-3 tablespoons
- Oregano for garnish - 1 pinch

Instructions:

1. Mix the oregano, ground cinnamon, cumin, coriander, salt, and allspice.
2. Combine the chicken thighs (cut into bite-sized pieces), oil, and shawarma spice mix. Coat the chicken evenly with the spice mixture.
3. Let the chicken marinate at room temperature for 30 minutes before cooking. If you have time, cover the bowl with plastic wrap and refrigerate the chicken overnight.
4. Preheat your air fryer to 170°C (350°F).
5. Place the chicken in the bottom of the air fryer basket in a single layer.
6. Cook the chicken for 12-15 minutes or until it is golden brown and cooked.
7. Whisk together the Greek yoghurt and lemon juice to make the yoghurt dressing.
8. To assemble the bowls, divide 2 cups of cauliflower rice among four bowls. Top each bowl with a handful of salad greens, a few slices of cucumber, halved cherry tomatoes, and a few olives.
9. Add the chicken shawarma to each bowl, then drizzle with the yoghurt dressing. You can also garnish with fresh herbs, chopped nuts, or a squeeze of lemon juice.

Nutrition Value:

Calories: 313 | Fat: 17g | Saturates: 7g | Carbs: 12g | Sugars: 5g | Fibre: 3g | Protein: 29g | Salt: 1.25g

ZUCCHINI CORN FRITTERS IN AIR FRYER

Preparation Time: 15 minutes | Cooking Time: 15 minutes | Servings: 10-12

Ingredients:

- Zucchini - 450 grams (about 2 medium zucchinis)
- Corn kernels, (canned or frozen) - 164 grams (1 cup)
- Grated parmesan cheese - 22 grams (¼ cup)
- Yellow onion, grated - 13 grams (¼ cup)
- Garlic, finely minced - 1 clove
- Dried parsley - 1 tablespoon
- Salt - 1 teaspoon
- freshly ground black pepper - ½ teaspoon
- dried basil - ½ teaspoon
- dried oregano - ½ teaspoon
- Paprika - ¼ teaspoon
- Eggs - 2
- Almond flour, or all-purpose flour - 120 grams (1 cup)
- Baking powder - 1 teaspoon
- Oil spray

Instructions:

1. Preheat your air fryer to 180°C (360°F).
2. Shred the zucchini using the large holes on a box grater, and keep it on a kitchen towel.
3. Wrap the kitchen towel around the zucchini and squeeze out excess water.
4. Add corn kernels, cheese, onion, garlic, parsley, salt, pepper, basil, oregano, paprika, and beaten eggs to the zucchini; stir to combine.
5. Add flour and baking powder, and stir until everything is well incorporated. Add more flour if the mixture is too runny. The drier the zucchini, the less flour you need.
6. Shape the mixture into 10 to 12 patties.
7. As an optional step, you can place the raw patties in the freezer for approximately 5 to 8 minutes to aid in maintaining their shape while cooking.
8. Grease the air fryer basket with cooking spray.
9. Working in batches and making sure not to crowd the air fryer basket, place the patties in the air fryer in a single layer and spray them with cooking spray.
10. Cook the patties for 6 minutes.
11. Flip over the patties, spray with cooking spray, and cook for 6 to 8 more minutes or until browned.
12. Remove from the air fryer and serve hot!

Nutrition Value:

Calories: 95 | Fat: 6g | Saturates: 1g | Carbs: 7g | Sugars: 2g | Fibre: 2g | Protein: 5g | Salt: 0.32g

CLASSIC AIR-FRIED ITALIAN ARANCINI

Preparation Time: 1 hour | Cooking Time: 12 minutes | Servings: 24 Arancinis

Ingredients:

- Chicken stock - 890 ml (3 ½ cups)
- Butter - 3 tablespoons
- Onion finely, chopped - 175 grams (¾ cup)
- Carnaroli or Arborio rice - 190 grams (1 cup)
- White wine dry - 120 ml (½ cup)
- Parmesan cheese, grated - 55 grams (½ cup)
- Heavy cream - 80 ml (⅓ cup)

- Basil fresh + chopped - 1 ½ tablespoons
- Salt and pepper, to taste
- Eggs - 3
- Mozzarella cheese cubed - 90 grams (½ cup)
- All-purpose flour - 60 grams (½ cup)
- Italian bread crumbs dry - 120 grams (1 cup)

Instructions:

1. Heat the chicken stock in a medium pot until it reaches a simmer. Then, remove the pot from the heat and place a lid on top to keep it warm. Set it aside.
2. In a pan, melt butter, and sauté onions until they are transparent around 4 minutes.
3. Add rice to the pan, stirring constantly. Cook until it is opaque, around 1 minute.
4. Pour wine into the pan and stir until the rice absorbs it.
5. While stirring, add the chicken stock to the pan in increments of ½ cup. Allow the liquid to soak in before adding more.
6. Cook for 20 minutes until the rice is tender and the risotto is creamy. The amount of stock needed may vary based on the heat and thickness of your pan.
7. Remove the pan from heat, and stir in the heavy cream, parmesan, and basil.
8. Try the risotto and add salt and pepper as per your preference.
9. Spread the risotto onto a plate and place it in the fridge to cool for 1 hour.
10. Stir one egg into the risotto until well incorporated.
11. Scoop the risotto and press a piece of cheese in the centre.
12. Roll the risotto into 24 tight balls using your hands and place them on a clean plate.
13. Prep 3 bowls: 1 for the flour, 1 for the 2 remaining eggs, and 1 for the breadcrumbs.
14. Dip each arancino in the flour, then dip it in the eggs and in the bread crumbs.
15. Spray both the arancini and air fryer tray with oil.
16. Cook at 200°C (400°F) for 12 minutes.
17. Serve immediately with tomato sauce!

Nutrition Value:

Calories: 122 | Fat: 5g | Saturates: 3g | Carbs: 14g | Sugars: 1g | Fibre: 1g | Protein: 5g | Salt: 0.19g

PERFECT STEAK IN AIR FRYER

Preparation Time: 5 minutes | Cooking Time: 10 minutes | Servings: 2

Ingredients:

- Rump steak, about 2.5 cm (225 grams) each - 2
- Vegetable oil - 2 teaspoons

- Salt, to taste
- Freshly cracked black pepper, to taste

For Garlic butter:

- Softened butter - 60 grams
- Large garlic, chopped - 2

- Parsley, chopped - 1 tablespoon
- Chives, chopped - 1 tablespoon

Instructions:

1. Make the garlic butter by combining softened butter, chopped garlic, parsley, and chive in a bowl or plate. Mix the ingredients thoroughly until well combined.
2. Once the garlic butter is ready, transfer it to clingfilm and store it in the refrigerator until needed.
3. Preheat the air fryer to 200°C (400°F) for 10 minutes before cooking the steak.
4. Pat the steak dry to remove excess moisture. Then, generously season the entire steak with salt and pepper.
5. Rub oil onto both sides of the steak to prevent it from sticking to the air fryer basket.
6. Grease the air fryer basket with oil to prevent the steak from sticking.
7. Place the seasoned steak in the air fryer and cook it for 8 to 10 minutes or until the desired doneness is achieved.
8. Flip the steak halfway through cooking to ensure it cooks evenly on both sides.
9. Once the steak cooks to your liking, remove it from the air fryer basket and put it on a plate.
10. Top the steak with the garlic butter prepared in the first step.
11. Cover the steak with tin foil for at least 5 minutes before serving, allowing the juices to absorb into the steak for a juicy and flavourful meal.
12. Serve the steak with your favourite sides, and enjoy your delicious steak!

Nutrition Value:

Calories: 569 | Fat: 39g | Saturates: 23g | Carbs: 1g | Sugars: 1g | Fibre: 1g | Protein: 50g | Salt: 0.35g

AIR FRIED BUTTERNUT SQUASH SOUP

Preparation Time: 15 minutes | Cooking Time: 40 minutes | Servings: 8

Ingredients:

- Diced Butternut Squash - 907 grams (2 pounds)
- Peeled Carrots, cut into sticks or roughly chopped - 340 grams (12 oz)
- Apple, cored and roughly chopped - 1
- Shallot, peeled and quartered - 1
- Olive Oil - 2 tablespoons

- Garlic Powder - 1 teaspoon
- Dried Rosemary - 1 teaspoon
- Black Pepper - ½ teaspoon
- Red Pepper Flakes - ¼ teaspoon
- Ground Sage - ¼ teaspoon
- Fresh garlic, peeled - 5 cloves

To add after roasting:

- Vegetable Broth (or your choice of broth) - 946 ml (4 cups)

- Lite Coconut Milk (or your choice of cream/milk) - 120 grams (½ cup)
- Kosher Salt - 2 teaspoons

Instructions:

1. In a large bowl, mix all the ingredients up to the ground sage. Add the mixture to an air fryer basket.
2. Air fry the vegetables for 40 minutes at 200°C (400°F), stirring occasionally. Halfway through cooking, add the garlic cloves to the basket to avoid burning them.
3. Once the vegetables are fork-tender, transfer them to a food processor or blender in batches. Gradually blend them with about 2 cups of broth.
4. Stir in the remaining broth, coconut milk, and salt until the soup is smooth.
5. If using a Ninja Foodi, turn on the "Keep Warm" function and add the soup to the pot. Alternatively, add the soup to a pot over low heat or a slow cooker to keep it warm.
6. Let the soup simmer for 10 to 15 minutes before serving to allow the flavours to develop.
7. Season the soup with salt and pepper to your desired taste. Serve with pepitas and top it with maple syrup, honey, or cream.

Nutrition Value:

Calories: 280 | Fat: 15.5g | Saturates: 2.5g | Carbs: 23g | Sugars: 12g | Fibre: 7g | Protein: 5g | Salt: 0.43g

NINJA AIR FRYER GREEK CHICKEN BOWL

Preparation Time: 10 minutes | Cooking Time: 16 minutes | Servings: 4

Ingredients:

For chicken and marinade:

- 225g boneless skinless chicken breasts - 2
- Olive oil - 2 tablespoons
- Dried oregano - 2 teaspoons
- Italian seasoning - 1 teaspoon
- Kosher salt - 1 teaspoon
- Ground black pepper - ½ teaspoon
- Juice of half a lemon

For bowls:

- Cooked cauliflower rice - 450 grams (2 cups)
- Cherry tomatoes rinsed and halved - 300 grams (1 pint)
- Sliced cucumbers English cucumbers recommended - 120 grams (1 cup)
- Sliced red onion - 60 grams (½ cup)
- Reduced fat feta crumbles - 56 grams (½ cup)
- Fresh chopped dill - 1 tablespoon
- Lemon wedges - 4
- Skinny tzatziki sauce - 1 batch

Instructions:

1. Mix the olive oil, oregano, Italian seasoning, salt, pepper, and lemon juice.
2. Toss the chicken breasts in the marinade and refrigerate for 30 minutes.
3. Meanwhile, prepare the tzatziki sauce if it hasn't been prepared yet.
4. Remove the refrigerated chicken from the bowl and discard the marinade.
5. Grease the bottom of the air fryer basket with olive oil spray.
6. Place the chicken into the greased air fryer basket and cook at 190°C (375°F) for 13 to 16 minutes, turning it over halfway through.
7. Take out the chicken from the air fryer and allow it to rest for 2 to 3 minutes.
8. Divide the cooked cauliflower rice, regular rice, or any grain between four bowls.
9. Next, divide the halved cherry tomatoes, sliced English cucumbers, and sliced red onions evenly between the four bowls.
10. Add one-quarter of the sliced and cooked chicken to the top of each bowl.
11. Spoon the homemade tzatziki sauce across the chicken and sprinkle 2 tablespoons of reduced-fat feta crumbles over each bowl.
12. Finally, garnish each bowl with fresh dill and serve with a lemon wedge on the side for added flavour. Serve, and enjoy

Nutrition Value:

Calories: 316 | Fat: 15g | Saturates: 4g | Carbs: 17g | Sugars: 7g | Fibre: 4g | Protein: 32g | Salt: 0.99g

CHICKEN BREAST IN NINJA AIR FRYER

Preparation Time: 10 minutes | Cooking Time: 17 minutes | Servings: 4

Ingredients:

- Brown sugar - 2 teaspoons
- Paprika - 1 teaspoon
- Dried oregano - 1 teaspoon
- Garlic powder - ½ teaspoon
- Onion powder - ¼ teaspoon
- Salt - ¼ teaspoon
- Black pepper - ⅛ teaspoon
- Boneless, skinless chicken breasts - 2
- Olive oil - 1 teaspoon

Instructions:

1. Prepare a spice mixture in a small bowl by combining the brown sugar, paprika, dried oregano, garlic powder, onion powder, salt, and pepper.
2. Stir or whisk the mixture until all the ingredients are well combined and evenly distributed.
3. Take your chicken breasts and pat them dry using paper towels to remove any excess moisture.
4. To achieve even cooking, place the chicken breasts in a zip-top bag or between two layers of parchment paper, and use a meat mallet or rolling pin to pound them to an even thickness.
5. Once the chicken has been pounded, rub olive oil over all sides of the chicken breasts to help the spice mixture adhere and keep the chicken moist during cooking.
6. Now, rub the spice mixture on both sides of the chicken, coating the chicken breasts evenly.
7. Preheat your air fryer to 200°C (400°F).
8. Once the air fryer is heated, place the chicken in the basket of the air fryer.
9. Cook the chicken at 200°C (400°F) for 8 minutes, then flip the chicken over and continue cooking for an additional 5 to 12 minutes, or until the internal temperature of the chicken reaches 75°C (165°F) at the thickest part of the breast. The cooking time may vary depending on the size of the chicken breasts and your air fryer.
10. Once the chicken has finished cooking, transfer it onto a plate.
11. Let it rest for 5 minutes to allow the juices to redistribute within the meat for a more tender and flavourful chicken.
12. Slice and serve!

Nutrition Value:

½ Chicken Breast: Calories: 85 | Fat: 3g | Saturates: 1g | Carbs: 3g | Sugars: 2g | Fibre: 1g | Protein: 12g | Salt: 0.21g

NINJA AIR FRYER STUFFED PORK CHOPS

Preparation Time: 10 minutes | Cooking Time: 18 minutes | Servings: 4

Ingredients:

- Bone-in pork rib chops (1 ½ to 2 inches thick) - 4
- Cooked box stuffing (you can use homemade as well) - 710 ml (3 cups)

- Salt, to taste
- Black pepper, to taste

Instructions:

1. Preheat your air fryer to 165°C (330°F) degrees.
2. Create a pocket in every pork chop by making a horizontal cut that goes almost to the bone.
3. Fill the pocket with the stuffing mixture using a spoon. Pack the stuffing tightly to avoid any gaps. You can secure the opening with toothpicks to keep them from falling out during cooking. Use approximately ¾ cups of stuffing per pork chop.
4. Season the pork chops thoroughly with salt and pepper to taste.
5. Arrange the stuffed pork chops in the air fryer in a single layer.
6. Cook the pork chops for 13 minutes on one side.
7. After 13 minutes, flip the pork chops over, spray them with oil, and cook them for another 5 to 6 minutes. This ensures that the pork chops are crispy on the outside and fully cooked on the inside. The pork chops are ready when their internal temperature reaches 65°C (150°F) at their thickest point.
8. Remove the pork chops from the air fryer.
9. Allow the pork chops to rest for 5 minutes to let the juices settle back into the meat.
10. Serve, and enjoy!

Cooking Tip:

- To cook frozen stuffed pork chops, preheat the air fryer to 165°C (330°F). Then, place the frozen stuffed pork chops in the air fryer and cook for 20 minutes. Flip the pork chops over and cook for 5 to 8 more minutes until they reach an internal temperature of 65°C (150°F).
- To reheat stuffed pork chops, preheat the air fryer to 175°C (350°F). Place the leftover pork chops in and air fry for about 5 minutes until they are warmed through.

Nutrition Value:

Calories: 608 | Fat: 38g | Saturates: 10g | Carbs: 38g | Sugars: 4g | Fibre: 2g | Protein: 28g | Salt: 1.14g

JUICY HAMBURGER IN AIR FRYER

Preparation Time: 10 minutes | Cooking Time: 12 minutes | Servings: 4

Ingredients:

- Lean ground beef - 455 grams (1 pound)
- Worcestershire sauce - 1 tablespoon
- Garlic powder - 1 teaspoon
- Onion powder - 1 teaspoon
- Salt and pepper, to taste
- Hamburger buns - 4
- Toppings of your choice, such as lettuce, tomato, onion, cheese, etc.

Instructions:

1. Prepare your air fryer by preheating it to 190°C (375°F).
2. In a large mixing bowl, add the ground beef, Worcestershire sauce, garlic powder, onion powder, salt, and pepper. Mix well, but avoid overworking the meat as it can make the burgers stiff.
3. Divide the mixture into four equal portions and shape them into patties about 3 to 4 inches in diameter. To prevent the beef patties from doming up while cooking, create a slight indentation or concave in the centre of each patty.
4. Then, put the patties into the air fryer basket, ensuring that there is sufficient space between them. Depending on the size of your air fryer, you may need to cook the patties in batches.
5. Cook the patties for 10 to 12 minutes, flipping them halfway through the cooking time to ensure that both sides are evenly baked.
6. Once the burgers are ready, remove them from the air fryer and let them rest for a few minutes.
7. Assemble your burgers by placing each patty on a hamburger bun, and pile on your desired toppings.
8. Enjoy your juicy hamburger!

Cooking Tip:

- Use a meat thermometer to make sure that the internal temperature reaches at least 70°C (160°F).
- If your air fryer has a tendency to stick to food, use a spritz or brush of olive oil on the air fryer basket to create a non-stick surface.

Nutrition Value:

Calories: 447 | Fat: 23g | Saturates: 9.2g | Carbs: 24g | Sugars: 3g | Fibre: 1g | Protein: 32g | Salt: 0.58g

SEAFOOD

TASTY GARLIC BUTTER AIR FRYER COD

Preparation Time: 10 minutes | Cooking Time: 10 minutes | Servings: 4

Ingredients:

- Cod loins - 4
- Butter, melted - 4 tablespoons
- Garlic cloves, minced - 6
- Lemon juice - 2 tablespoons (1 lemon)
- Dried dill - 1 teaspoon
- Salt - ½ teaspoon

Instructions:

1. Preheat your air fryer to 190°C (370°F).
2. Mix the melted butter, minced garlic, lemon juice, dill, and salt in a small bowl until well combined.
3. Take a cod loin, and coat it thoroughly with the butter mixture using a brush. Lightly press the garlic onto the cod so it adheres well during cooking. Repeat the same process with the remaining cod pieces.
4. Place all the cod loins into the air fryer basket in a single layer, ensuring they are not touching.
5. Set the air fryer temperature to 10 minutes.
6. Once the set time elapses, carefully remove the cooked cod from the air fryer using tongs or a spatula.
7. If you wish, garnish the cod with more lemon juice or butter before serving.
8. Serve the air fryer garlic butter cod with your favourite side dishes, such as steamed vegetables or rice.

Nutrition Value:

Calories: 302 | Fat: 13g | Saturates: 8g | Carbs: 3g | Sugars: 0g | Fibre: 1g | Protein: 42g | Salt: 0.51g

AIR FRYER TENDER FURIKAKE SALMON

Preparation Time: 5 minutes | Cooking Time: 10 minutes | Servings: 3

Ingredients:

- Mayonnaise - 125 grams (½ cup)
- Shoyu - 1 tablespoon
- Salmon fillet - (455 grams) 1 pound
- Salt and pepper, to taste
- Furikake - 2 tablespoon

Instructions:

1. Preheat your air fryer to 200°C (400°F).
2. In a small bowl, add the mayonnaise and shoyu. Mix until well combined and set aside.
3. Pat dry the salmon fillet using a paper towel. Sprinkle and season both sides of the fillet with salt and pepper. If cooking with the skin intact, place the fillet skin side down.
4. Add the mayonnaise and shoyu mixture in an even layer on top of the salmon fillet. Sprinkle the furikake over the mayonnaise.
5. Spray the air fryer basket with non-stick cooking spray. Place the salmon fillet in the basket, skin side down.
6. Cook the salmon in the air fryer for 8 to 10 minutes or until it is flaky and cooked to the inside.
7. Carefully remove the cooked salmon from the air fryer using tongs or a spatula.
8. If you wish, garnish the salmon with additional furikake or chopped scallions.
9. Serve the air fryer furikake salmon hot, and enjoy!

Nutrition Value:

Calories: 578 | Fat: 47g | Saturates: 8g | Carbs: 2g | Sugars: 1g | Fibre: 1g | Protein: 34g | Salt: 0.56g

NINJA AIR FRYER SEA SCALLOPS

Preparation Time: 10 minutes | Cooking Time: 20 minutes | Servings: 2

Ingredients:

- Large sea scallops, cleaned and patted very dry - 8
- Ground pepper - ¼ teaspoon
- Salt - ⅛ teaspoon
- Cooking spray
- Extra-virgin olive oil - 60 ml (¼ cup)
- Flat-leaf parsley, finely chopped - 2 tablespoons
- Capers, finely chopped - 2 teaspoons
- Lemon zest, finely grated - 1 teaspoon
- Garlic, finely chopped - ½ teaspoon
- Lemon wedges

Instructions:

1. To prepare the scallops, start by rinsing them under cold water and drying them with paper towels.
2. Next, sprinkle both sides of the scallops with salt and black pepper and season thoroughly.
3. Coat the air fryer basket with cooking spray to prevent sticking.
4. Add the seasoned scallops to the air fryer basket, arranging them in a single layer without overcrowding.
5. Coat the scallops with cooking spray to ensure they crisp up during cooking.
6. Preheat the air fryer to 200°C (400°F), then place the basket with the scallops inside.
7. Cook the scallops until their internal temperature reaches 50°C (120°F), which should take around 6 minutes.
8. While the scallops are cooking, prepare the garnish by mixing olive oil, minced parsley, capers, lemon zest, and minced garlic in a small bowl.
9. Once the scallops are done, remove the basket from the air fryer and drizzle the prepared garnish over the top.
10. Serve immediately with lemon wedges on the side!

Nutrition Value:

Calories: 348 | Fat: 30g | Saturates: 4g | Carbs: 5g | Sugars: 1g | Fibre: 1g | Protein: 14g | Salt: 0.66g

KETO FRIED SHRIMP IN NINJA AIR FRYER

Preparation Time: 5 minutes | Cooking Time: 10 minutes | Servings: 8

Ingredients:

- Large shrimp peeled and deveined - 25
- Almond flour - 83 grams (⅔ cup)
- Eggs - 3
- Ground black pepper - 1 tablespoon
- Smoked paprika - 1 teaspoon
- Lemon pepper - 1 teaspoon (optional)

Instructions:

1. Preheat your air fryer to 200°C (400°F).
2. Prepare the air fryer basket by spraying it with non-stick cooking spray to prevent the shrimp from sticking and help them cook evenly.
3. Arrange two bowls on your work surface. In one bowl, mix the almond flour, paprika, lemon pepper, and ground black pepper. In the second bowl, whip the eggs together.
4. Dip each shrimp into the egg mixture first. Then dip the shrimp into the almond flour mixture, pressing the coating onto the shrimp to make sure it sticks. Set the coated shrimp aside on a wire rack.
5. Once you've coated all the shrimp, add them to the preheated air fryer basket in a single layer, making sure they're not touching each other.
6. Cook the shrimp for 10 to 12 minutes at 200°C (400°F), flipping them halfway through the cooking time.
7. Once the shrimp are golden brown on all sides, remove them from the air fryer basket and place them on a serving platter.
8. Serve the crispy air-fried sea scallops immediately with your favourite dipping sauce.

Cooking Tip: You can keep leftover fried shrimp in the refrigerator for up to 2 days. To reheat, place them in the air fryer basket and cook at 200°C (400°F) for 2 minutes, adding an extra minute if necessary.

Nutrition Value:

Calories: 98 | Fat: 7g | Saturates: 1g | Carbs: 1g | Sugars: 1g | Fibre: 1g | Protein: 8g | Salt: 0.17g

AIR-FRIED CRAB LEGS

Preparation Time: 15 minutes | Cooking Time: 10 minutes | Servings: 2

Ingredients:

- Crab legs - 455 grams (1 pound)
- Butter - 2 tablespoons
- Garlic clove, minced - 1
- Salt and pepper, to taste
- Lemon Wedges

Instructions:

1. Preheat your air fryer to 190°C (380°F).
2. While the air fryer is preheating, rinse the crab legs under cold water and pat them dry with paper towels.
3. Once the air fryer is heated, place the crab legs in the air fryer basket. Make sure to arrange them in a single layer, leaving some space between them.
4. You can melt the butter either on the stovetop or in a dish that's microwave-safe. If using a microwave, heat the butter in 15-second intervals until melted. If using the stovetop, melt the butter over low heat.
5. Add minced garlic to the melted butter and stir to combine.
6. Drizzle the garlic butter over the crab legs, coating them evenly. Use a brush or a spoon to spread the butter over the crab legs, if necessary.
7. Season the crab legs with salt and pepper to taste. You can use as much or as little salt and pepper as you like.
8. Place the basket in the air fryer and cook the crab legs for 5 to 7 minutes. The exact cooking time may vary depending on the size and thickness of the crab legs, as well as the wattage of your air fryer. After 5 minutes, examine the crab legs to ensure they are hot to the inside and the butter is bubbling. If not, continue cooking for 1 to 2 more minutes.
9. Once the crab legs are done, remove the basket from the air fryer and transfer the crab legs to a serving dish.
10. Serve the crab legs hot with lemon wedges. Squeeze them over the crab legs to add a bright, citrusy flavour that complements the sweetness of the crab meat. Enjoy!

Nutrition Value:

Calories: 215 | Fat: 11g | Saturates: 5g | Carbs: 0g | Sugars: 0g | Fibre: 0g | Protein: 25g | Salt: 0.58g

HOMEMADE AIR FRYER FRESH FILLETS

Preparation Time: 10 minutes | Cooking Time: 15 minutes | Servings: 3

Ingredients:

- White fish fillets - 454 grams (1 pound)
- Kosher salt, to taste
- Black pepper, to taste
- Garlic powder - 1 teaspoon
- Paprika - 1 teaspoon
- Bread crumbs - 60-120 grams (1-2 cups)
- Egg - 1

Instructions:

1. Preheat the air fryer to 190°C (380°F) for 4 minutes.
2. If using frozen fillets, make sure to thaw them first. Cut fish fillets in half in even sizes so they cook evenly. Pat the fillets dry.
3. Lightly oil the fillets and then season with salt, black pepper, garlic powder, and paprika.
4. Put the bread crumbs in a shallow bowl. In another bowl, beat the eggs.
5. Dip the fillets in the egg, then dredge the fillets in the breadcrumbs. Gently press fillets into the bowl of bread crumbs so that they stick to the fillets. Repeat this process for all fish pieces.
6. Line the air fryer basket or tray with perforated parchment paper. (If you don't have perforated parchment paper, simply coat the air fryer basket with oil spray.)
7. Generously spray all sides of the breaded fillets with oil spray to coat any dry spots, and put them into the air fryer basket.
8. Air fry at 190°C (380°F) for 8 to 14 minutes, depending on the size and thickness of your fillets.
9. After 6 minutes, flip the fillets. Lightly spray oil on any dry spots, then continue cooking for the remaining time or until they are crispy brown and the fish is cooked.
10. Enjoy your crispy air-fried fish fillet with a dipping sauce such as classic tartar sauce, tangy mustard, creamy aioli, or any other dip.

Nutrition Value:

Calories: 314 | Fat: 6g | Saturates: 2g | Carbs: 27g | Sugars: 2g | Fibre: 1g | Protein: 37g | Salt: 1.14g

AIR FRYER BREADED OYSTER BITES

Preparation Time: 15 minutes | Cooking Time: 8 minutes | Servings: 6

Ingredients:

- Oysters - 2 cans, 226 grams (8 ounces) each
- Flour - 60 grams (½ cup)
- Cajun seasoning - 1 teaspoon
- Salt - 1 teaspoon
- Pepper - ½ teaspoon
- Eggs - 2
- Hot sauce - 3 tablespoons
- Panko bread crumbs - 120 grams (2 cups)
- Lemon - 1

Instructions:

1. Begin by draining the oysters and placing them on a paper towel to pat them dry.
2. Mix together the flour, Cajun seasoning, salt, and pepper in a shallow bowl.
3. In a separate bowl, whisk together the eggs and hot sauce until they are well combined.
4. Prepare a third bowl and add the Panko breadcrumbs into it.
5. Turn each oyster in the flour mixture, one at a time, coating it evenly.
6. Next, dip the flour-coated oyster into the egg mixture, again making sure to coat it evenly.
7. Finally, dredge the oyster in the Panko breadcrumbs, lightly pressing to help the breading stick.
8. Spray the air fryer basket with non-stick spray and arrange the coated oysters in a single layer in the basket.
9. Cook the oysters in the air fryer at 175°C (350°F) for four minutes.
10. After 4 minutes, gently shake the basket to ensure the oysters cook evenly.
11. Continue cooking for four more minutes until the oysters are golden brown and crispy.
12. Once done, remove the oysters from the air fryer and serve them with a squeeze of lemon on top.

Nutrition Value:

Calories: 145 | Fat: 3g | Saturates: 1g | Carbs: 25g | Sugars: 2g | Fibre: 2g | Protein: 6g | Salt: 0.73g

WHOLE FISH IN NINJA AIR FRYER

Preparation Time: 30 minutes | Cooking Time: 30 minutes | Servings: 2

Ingredients:

- Large bream, gutted and de-scaled - 2
- Seafood seasoning - 2 tablespoon
- Jerk seasoning paste - ½ teaspoon
- Paprika - 1 teaspoon
- Lime juice - 1 tablespoon
- Olive oil - 2 tablespoon
- Mixed vegetables, tightly packed - 250-364 grams (2-3 cups)

Instructions:

1. Place the fish on a chopping board or another clean working surface.
2. Use kitchen scissors to trim off the dorsal and pectoral fins of the fish and discard them.
3. Use a sharp knife to make 3 to 4 diagonal cuts on each side of the fish, leaving a 3 to 4 cm gap between each line. Be careful not to cut too deep into the fish's cavity.
4. Mix the olive oil, lime juice, jerk seasoning paste, and seafood seasoning in a small bowl. If the paste is too thick, add some water to thin it out.
5. Before applying the mixture to the fish, do a taste test to see if you want to add more pink salt and black pepper.
6. Use your hands or a pastry brush to thoroughly coat the fish with the wet rub, including the cuts and the cavity.
7. Leave the fish to marinate for 1 to 2 hours or overnight in the refrigerator if you have time.
8. Place some parchment paper or a liner in the basket and transfer the fish into it.
9. Set the air fryer time for 25 to 30 minutes and the temperature to 190°C (375°F).
10. Halfway through the cooking time, turn the fish over gently.
11. Ten minutes before the finishing time, add the vegetables into the basket.
12. Once the set time elapses and everything is cooked, sprinkle the vegetables with the seafood seasoning and serve.

Cooking Tip: You may use any other whole fish of your choice for this recipe, such as parrot fish, doctor fish, butterfish, snapper, red mullet, sprats, or any other suitable fish.

Nutrition Value:

Calories: 665 | Fat: 28g | Saturates: 2g | Carbs: 19g | Sugars: 1g | Fibre: 6g | Protein: 83g | Salt: 0.73g

AIR-FRIED LOBSTER WITH CREAM SAUCE

Preparation Time: 10 minutes | Cooking Time: 7 minutes | Servings: 2

Ingredients:

- Fresh lobster tails, each weighing about 170 grams (6 ounces) - 2
- Butter, cubed - 3 tablespoons
- Salt and pepper, to taste
- Shallots, finely diced - 1 tablespoon
- Garlic cloves, minced - 2
- Chopped parsley, plus more for garnish - 2 tablespoons
- Heavy cream - 75 grams (⅓ cup)
- Grated parmesan cheese - 1 tablespoon
- Lemon juice - 1 tablespoon l
- Lemon wedges, to serve

Instructions:

1. Thaw the lobster tails if they are frozen by running them under cold water.
2. Place the lobster tails on a cutting board or another clean working surface.
3. Take a pair of kitchen shears, and cut straight down the centre of the top of the lobster shell towards the fins of the tail, but be careful not to cut through the fin.
4. Use a spoon to loosen the meat by running it along the shell.
5. Carefully lift the lobster meat off the shell's bottom while keeping it attached.
6. With a knife, cut halfway the meat down to the centre. Do not cut all the way through.
7. Melt a tablespoon of butter and brush it over the lobster tails.
8. Season the lobster tails with salt and pepper for added taste.
9. Cook the lobster tails in the air fryer at 190°C (380°F) for 5 to 7 minutes.
10. Meanwhile, prepare the sauce by melting two tablespoons of butter in a pan.
11. Add the shallots to the pan and fry them for one minute.
12. Toss in the garlic and parsley and cook for 20 seconds while stirring.
13. Turn down the heat to medium-low and stir the heavy cream into the skillet.
14. Add the parmesan cheese and bring the sauce to a simmer; cook for 1 to 2 minutes or until slightly thickened.
15. Whisk in the lemon juice for added flavour.
16. Taste the sauce and adjust the seasoning with salt and pepper as you desire.
17. Remove the sauce from the heat.
18. Once the lobster tails are cooked, serve them with the delicious sauce on the side!

Nutrition Value:

Calories: 356 | Fat: 33g | Saturates: 20g | Carbs: 4g | Sugars: 2g | Fibre: 0.4g | Protein: 13g | Salt: 0.46g

KING PRAWNS IN NINJA AIR FRYER

Preparation Time: 5 minutes | Cooking Time: 8 minutes | Servings: 2

Ingredients:

- King prawns, peeled - 400 grams
- Onion, finely chopped - ½
- Garlic cloves, finely chopped - 2
- Olive oil - 2 tablespoons
- Fresh parsley, finely chopped - 15 grams
- Sea salt and black pepper, to serve
- Lemon juice, to serve

Instructions:

1. Peel the prawns and remove the heads, leaving the tails intact. Rinse them thoroughly under running water and pat dry with paper towels.
2. In a bowl, mix the prawns, finely chopped onions, minced garlic, chopped parsley, sea salt and black pepper. Leave to marinate for about 15 minutes to allow the flavours to meld.
3. After 15 minutes, drizzle the olive oil in the bowl and mix everything.
4. Transfer the prawn mixture to the air fryer basket, spreading them out in an even layer.
5. Cook the prawns in the air fryer at 220°C (430°F) for 8 minutes. Keep an eye on them and ensure they turn a nice, rich pink colour.
6. Once the prawns are cooked, transfer the cooked prawns to a serving dish and garnish with the lemon wedges.
7. Squeeze fresh lemon juice over the prawns to add a zesty, citrusy flavour.
8. Serve the prawns immediately while they're still hot, and enjoy!

Cooking Tip:

- Add a twist to the dish by incorporating coconut, Panko breadcrumbs, or Mexican seasoning.
- Serve the prawns with rice or salad, or use them as filling in tacos or a burrito bowl.
- You can enhance the recipe with chopped bell peppers and courgettes to increase the veggie content.
- If using frozen prawns, ensure they are defrosted, and any excess liquid is removed.

Nutrition Value:

Calories: 152 | Fat: 14g | Saturates: 2g | Carbs: 7g | Sugars: 2g | Fibre: 2g | Protein: 1g | Salt: 0.07g

SIDE DISHES

STUFFED TOMATOES IN AIR FRYER

Preparation Time: 10 minutes | Cooking Time: 7 minutes | Servings: 2

Ingredients:

- Medium tomatoes - 4
- Olive oil, as needed
- Cooked brown rice - 195 grams (1 cup)
- Parmesan cheese, freshly grated - 30 grams (☐ cup)
- Crumbled goat cheese - 28 grams (¼ cup)
- Chopped toasted walnuts - 30 grams (¼ cup)
- Chopped fresh basil - 2 tablespoons
- Garlic cloves, minced - 2
- Italian-seasoned bread crumbs - 20 grams (¼ cup)
- Olive oil - 1 tablespoon

Instructions:

1. Prepare the tomatoes by washing and drying them. Cut off the top of each tomato with a sharp knife and scoop out the flesh using a small spoon, being careful not to break the sides or bottom of the tomato. Leave about ¼ to ½ inch thick walls to hold the filling. You can save the tomato tops and flesh for other recipes.
2. Brush the bottom of an air fryer basket with olive oil to prevent the tomatoes from sticking.
3. In a medium bowl, mix cooked rice, grated Parmesan cheese, crumbled goat cheese, chopped walnuts, one tablespoon of chopped basil, and minced garlic.
4. In a separate small bowl, combine bread crumbs and one tablespoon of olive oil.
5. Fill each tomato with the rice mixture until they are full but not overflowing. Sprinkle the breadcrumb mixture on top of each tomato.
6. Place the stuffed tomatoes into the prepared air fryer basket.
7. Set the air fryer temperature to 190°C (370°F) for about 15 minutes.
8. Check the tomatoes occasionally to make sure they are cooking evenly. The tomatoes should be tender, the filling heated through, and the topping golden brown when done.
9. Once the set time elapses, remove the tomatoes from the air fryer and garnish with the remaining chopped basil.
10. Serve immediately and enjoy!

Nutrition Value:

Calories: 255 | Fat: 27g | Saturates: 4g | Carbs: 23g | Sugars: 4g | Fibre: 3.2g | Protein: 9g | Salt: 2.03g

EASY FLUFFY BISCUITS IN AIR FRYER

Preparation Time: 10 minutes | Cooking Time: 10 minutes | Servings: 10

Ingredients:

- All-purpose flour - 250 grams (2 cups)
- Baking powder - 3 teaspoons
- Salt - ½ teaspoon
- Cold butter, cut into little squares - 7 tablespoons
- Cold milk - 250 ml (1 cup)
- Butter, melted - 2 tablespoons

Instructions:

1. Stir the flour, baking powder, and salt in a large mixing bowl until they are well mixed.
2. Cut the cold butter into small cubes and add them to the mixing bowl. Blend the butter into the flour mixture until it resembles coarse gravel.
3. Pour in the milk and stir until it forms a dough. Don't overwork the dough, or the biscuits will be tough. To achieve the perfect texture, stir the dough just enough to combine the ingredients.
4. Scoop out ten even portions of dough with a spoon. If you want bigger biscuits, you can use a larger spoon.
5. Place the biscuits in the air fryer basket, spacing them apart. Depending on the size of your air fryer, you may need to cook the biscuits in two batches.
6. Set the temperature to 200°C (400°F) and cook the biscuits for 8 minutes.
7. After 8 minutes, open the air fryer basket and brush melted butter on top of the biscuits to add flavour and help the biscuits turn a beautiful golden brown.
8. Close the basket and continue cooking until the biscuits are lightly golden brown on top, for about 1 to 2 more minutes. The exact cooking time will depend on the air fryer and the size of the biscuits. Check them frequently to ensure they don't burn.
9. Once the biscuits are cooked to perfection, remove them from the air fryer and let them cool slightly.
10. Serve them hot with butter or jam, and enjoy!

Nutrition Value:

Calories: 197 | Fat: 11g | Saturates: 7g | Carbs: 21g | Sugars: 1g | Fibre: 1g | Protein: 3g | Salt: 0.34g

AIR FRIED HASH BROWNS

Preparation Time: 2 minutes | Cooking Time: 23 minutes | Servings: 4

Ingredients:

- Frozen shredded hash brown potatoes - 450 grams (16 oz)
- Garlic powder - ½ teaspoon
- Kosher salt, to taste
- Black pepper, to taste

Instructions:

1. Preheat your air fryer to 190°C (370°F).
2. Take the frozen hash browns and spread them out in a single layer inside the air fryer basket. The hash browns should not be piled on top of each other, which can cause them to cook unevenly.
3. Spray the top of the hash brown layer with olive oil to help them get crispy. Then, sprinkle garlic powder, salt, and pepper on top of the hash browns to taste.
4. Cook the hash browns for 18 minutes.
5. Open the air fryer, stir the hash browns and carefully flip them with a spatula so that both sides are evenly crispy.
6. Spray the hash browns with olive oil again and continue to air fry for about 5 more minutes or until they're golden brown and crispy to your liking.
7. Once the hash browns are ready, remove them from the air fryer and transfer them to a serving plate.
8. Season with some more salt and pepper if desired, and serve immediately.

Cooking Tip:

- The exact cooking time may vary depending on the size of your air fryer and the thickness of the hash browns. So, keep an eye on them to avoid burning them.
- To reheat the hash browns, preheat your air fryer to 190°C (370°F). Place the leftover hash browns in the air fryer and cook for 3 to 5 minutes until they are warmed and crisped thoroughly.

Nutrition Value:

Calories: 311 | Fat: 19g | Saturates: 3g | Carbs: 33g | Sugars: 1g | Fibre: 3g | Protein: 3g | Salt: 0.72g

SMOKY SHISHITO PEPPERS IN AIR FRYER

Preparation Time: 7 minutes | Cooking Time: 8 minutes | Servings: 4

Ingredients:

- Shishito peppers - 225 grams (8 ounces)
- Avocado oil spray
- Salt, to taste

Instructions:

1. Begin by washing the shishito peppers and thoroughly drying them. Do not remove the stems! They add flavour and make them easier to handle.
2. Once they are clean and dry, spritz them with the avocado oil spray.
3. Place the shishito peppers in a single layer in the basket or tray of your air fryer.
4. Set the air fryer to 200°C (400°F) and the timer for 8 minutes.
5. Once the timer beeps, carefully remove the shishito peppers from the air fryer using tongs and transfer them to a plate or bowl. They should be blistered with dark charred areas.
6. Sprinkle the shishito peppers with salt as desired.
7. Serve the shishito peppers immediately or with your favourite dips!

Cooking Tip: While the shishito peppers are cooking, you may hear popping and hissing sounds. Don't worry if this happens; it's normal. The peppers should not explode but just expand as they cook.

Nutrition Value:

Calories: 45 | Fat: 3.5g | Saturates: 0.5g | Carbs: 3g | Sugars: 2g | Fibre: 2g | Protein: 1g | Salt: 0.39g

AIR FRYER DUMPLINGS AT HOME

Preparation Time: 20 minutes | Cooking Time: 10 minutes | Servings: 30-40 dumplings

Ingredients:

- Dumpling wrappers - 1 package (usually contains 30-40 wrappers)
- Ground pork or chicken - 455 grams (1 pound)
- Ginger, grated - 1 tablespoon
- Garlic cloves, minced - 3
- Soy sauce - 2 tablespoons
- Sesame oil - 1 tablespoon
- Cornstarch - 1 tablespoon
- Scallions. chopped - 20 grams (¼ cup)
- Cilantro, chopped - 15 grams (¼ cup)
- Black pepper - ¼ teaspoon
- Egg, beaten - 1
- Cooking spray

Instructions:

1. In a large bowl, mix together the ground pork or chicken, grated ginger, minced garlic, soy sauce, sesame oil, cornstarch, chopped scallions, chopped cilantro, black pepper, and beaten egg. Mix well until all ingredients are well combined.
2. Take a dumpling wrapper and place a small spoonful of the filling in the centre. Do not overfill the wrapper, as this will make it difficult to seal.
3. Moisten the edges of the wrapper by dipping your finger in water. Fold the wrapper in half and seal the edges by pinching them together. Repeat this entire process until all the filling is used.
4. Preheat your air fryer to 175°C (350°F) for 5 minutes.
5. Spray the air fryer basket with cooking spray. Place the dumplings in the basket, ensuring they are not too crowded.
6. Spray the tops of the dumplings with cooking oil.
7. Cook the dumplings for 8 to 10 minutes, flipping them halfway through cooking, until they are golden brown and crispy.
8. Serve the dumplings hot with soy sauce or your favourite dipping sauce.

Nutrition Value:

Calories: 200 | Fat: 8g | Saturates: 2g | Carbs: 19g | Sugars: 1g | Fibre: 1g | Protein: 12g | Salt: 0.4g

SWEET POTATO TOTS IN AIR FRYER

Preparation Time: 10 minutes | Cooking Time: 12 minutes | Servings: 25 tots

Ingredients:

- Sweet potato puree - 470 ml (2 cups)
- Salt - ½ teaspoon
- Cumin - ½ teaspoon
- Coriander - ½ teaspoon
- Panko breadcrumbs or regular breadcrumbs - 60 grams (½ cup)
- Spray oil

Instructions:

1. Preheat your air fryer to 200°C (390°F).
2. In a large bowl, mix the sweet potato puree, salt, cumin, coriander, and breadcrumbs.
3. Form the mixture into one tablespoon tots (you can use a cookie scoop) and arrange them on a plate.
4. Spray the tots with spray oil and move them around to coat the bottoms with oil too.
5. Carefully arrange the tots on the air fryer basket in a neat line. You may need to cook the tots in 2 to 3 batches.
6. Cook the tots for 6 to 7 minutes and then carefully flip them over. If the tots feel too soft and mushy when you flip them, leave them for a few more minutes.
7. Cook for 5 to 7 more minutes until both sides are crispy but not burned.
8. Serve the hot sweet potato tots with guacamole, ketchup, or chipotle mayo.

To prepare ahead and freeze the sweet potato tots:

1. Form the tots and arrange them on a baking sheet. Freeze them for several hours.
2. Transfer the tots to a large freezer bag and remove as much air as possible.
3. When ready to cook, preheat the air fryer to 200°C (390°F).
4. Spray the frozen tots with spray oil, coating all sides evenly.
5. Carefully arrange the tots on the air fryer basket in a neat line.
6. Cook the tots for 9 to 10 minutes and then carefully flip them over. If the tots feel too soft and mushy when you flip them, leave them for a few more minutes.
7. Cook for approximately five more minutes, until both sides are crispy but not burned.
8. Serve the hot sweet potato tots with guacamole, ketchup, or chipotle mayo.

Nutrition Value:

Calories: 26 | Fat: 0g | Saturates: 0g | Carbs: 6g | Sugars: 2g | Fibre: 2g | Protein: 1g | Salt: 0.32g

AIR-FRIED CRISPY POTATO WEDGES

Preparation Time: 10 minutes | Cooking Time: 12 minutes | Servings: 25 tots

Ingredients:

- Small russet potatoes - 4 (680 grams)
- Olive oil - 1 tablespoon
- Paprika - ½ teaspoon
- Onion powder - ½ teaspoon
- Garlic powder - ½ teaspoon
- Salt - ½ teaspoon

Instructions:

1. Cut the potatoes in half and then each half in half again. Finally, cut each quarter on an angle to create 8 potato wedges from one potato.
2. Soak the potato wedges in a bowl of cold water and leave them to sit for 15 to 30 minutes. This helps remove starches from the surface of the potatoes and soaks the insides with moisture, preventing them from drying out in the air fryer.
3. Shake off excess water and arrange the potato wedges on a clean kitchen towel. Dab with a second towel to remove extra moisture from the surface of the potato.
4. Toss the potato wedges in oil to coat, then in paprika, onion powder, garlic powder, and salt. Mix until coated evenly.
5. Heat the air fryer to 200°C (400°F) for 5 minutes.
6. Lay the potato wedges cut side down in the air fryer and cook for 7 minutes. Flip the wedges and air fry the other side for 3 to 5 more minutes.
7. The potatoes are ready when the tops are crispy and the insides are soft. You can break one open and taste it.
8. Serve with sour cream or ketchup on the side. Enjoy!

Nutrition Value:

8 wedges: Calories: 168 | Fat: 4g | Saturates: 1g | Carbs: 31g | Sugars: 1g | Fibre: 2g | Protein: 4g | Salt: 0.3g

ROASTED VEGGIES IN AIR FRYER

Preparation Time: 10 minutes | Cooking Time: 15 minutes | Servings: 4

Ingredients:

Firm vegetables:

- Medium sweet potato - 1
- Medium potato - 1

- Chopped butternut squash (yellow squash, or pumpkin) - 120 grams (1 cup)
- Medium carrot - 1

Soft vegetables:

- Broccoli - ½ head
- Medium red onion - 1
- Olive oil (or avocado oil) - 3 tablespoons

- Kosher salt - 1 teaspoon
- Seasoning - 1 teaspoon

Instructions:

1. Prepare the potatoes, sweet potatoes, and squash by washing and peeling them. Cut them into chunks that are 1 to 2 inches in size.
2. Place the cut vegetables into a bowl of cold water and let them soak for 5 minutes.
3. Wash and peel the remaining vegetables, and cut them into 1 to 2-inch chunks.
4. Preheat your air fryer to 180°C (360°F).
5. Drain the soaked vegetables and pat them dry with a paper towel.
6. In a large bowl, mix olive oil, salt, and your choice of seasoning. Add the firm vegetables (potatoes, sweet potatoes, squash, etc.) to the bowl and toss them to coat with the seasoning.
7. Place the seasoned firm vegetables in the air fryer basket and air fry for 5 minutes.
8. While the firm vegetables are cooking, add the soft vegetables (such as zucchini or bell peppers) to the bowl with the oil/seasoning mix. Toss them to coat with the seasoning.
9. After 5 minutes, gently shake the air fryer basket to redistribute the vegetables. Then, add the soft vegetables on top of the firm vegetables in the basket.
10. Air fry for 10 to 15 more minutes, shaking the basket every 5 minutes. Once the vegetables are tender or cooked to your liking, remove them from the air fryer and serve them hot. Enjoy!

Nutrition Value:

Calories: 207 | Fat: 11g | Saturates: 1g | Carbs: 27g | Sugars: 6g | Fibre: 6g | Protein: 4g | Salt: 9.5g

AIR FRYER FLUFFY DINNER ROLLS

Preparation Time: 10 minutes | Cooking Time: 12 minutes | Servings: 7

Ingredients:

- Roux starter
- Bread flour - 2 tablespoons
- Water - 6 tablespoons
- Bread dough
- Bread flour - 300 grams (about 2 cups, plus 2 tablespoons)

- Milk - 120 ml (½ cup)
- Unsalted butter, melted - 2 tablespoons
- Instant yeast - 2 teaspoons
- Egg - 1
- Sugar - 2 tablespoons
- Salt - 1 teaspoon

Instructions:

1. In a small saucepan, combine water and bread flour together until there are no lumps. Whisk the mixture continuously for 3 to 5 minutes over low heat until it thickens into a glue-like consistency. Let it cool and set it aside.
2. In a large bowl, mix bread flour, sugar, yeast, and salt with a wooden spoon.
3. Whisk an egg and add ¾ of it to the cooled flour mixture in the saucepan. Stir until the mixture is smooth.
4. Melt butter in a saucepan or microwave and pour it into the big bowl with the flour mixture. Add the milk and the flour mixture from the saucepan as well. Knead the ingredients together until they form an elastic dough that is no longer sticky.
5. Place the dough in an Instant Pot set to yoghurt and leave it with the lid closed for 30 minutes to proof.
6. After 30 minutes, knead the dough by hand and divide it into 7 equal parts. Roll out each part into a rectangle and fold it like wrapping a gift. Then shape them into balls and put them in a pizza pan. Cover the pan with a clean kitchen towel or plastic wrap and let it rise again for 40 minutes.
7. Preheat the air fryer to 200°C (400°F) for about 3 minutes.
8. Glaze the tops of the buns with the remaining whisked egg.
9. Place the pan in the air fryer and bake the milk bread for 12 to 15 minutes or until golden brown. Check the bread halfway through the baking time.
10. Remove the pan from the air fryer and set it on a cooling rack for 5 minutes.
11. Serve with your dinner or a soup!

Nutrition Value:

Calories: 229 | Fat: 5g | Saturates: 3g | Carbs: 38g | Sugars: 4g | Fibre: 1g | Protein: 7g | Salt: 0.32g

SNACKS

PEANUT BUTTER COOKIES IN AIR FRYER

Preparation Time: 10 minutes | Cooking Time: 8-10 minutes | Servings: 12-15

Ingredients:

- All-purpose flour - 120 grams (1 cup)
- baking soda - ½ teaspoon
- Salt - ¼ teaspoon
- Unsalted butter, softened - 113 grams (½ cup)
- Granulated sugar - 100 grams (½ cup)
- Brown sugar - 100 grams (½ cup)
- Creamy peanut butter - 125 grams (½ cup)
- Egg - 1
- Vanilla extract - 1 teaspoon

Instructions:

1. Preheat your air fryer to 175°C (350°F).
2. Blend the flour, baking soda, and salt in a medium mixing bowl. Set aside.
3. In a separate large bowl, cream together the softened butter, granulated sugar, brown sugar, and peanut butter until the mixture is light and fluffy.
4. Crack in the egg, add the vanilla extract, and mix until well combined.
5. Stir in the flour mixture slowly until just combined. Be careful not to overmix.
6. Roll the dough into small balls, about 1-2 tablespoons in size, and place them onto a baking sheet lined with parchment paper.
7. Use a fork to press down on the cookies and make a crisscross pattern on the top.
8. Place the cookies into the preheated air fryer and cook for 8 to 10 minutes or until they are golden brown.
9. Once the cookies are done, carefully remove the baking sheet from the air fryer and allow the cookies to cool for a few minutes on the sheet before transferring them to a wire rack to cool completely.
10. Enjoy your soft, chewy peanut butter cookies as a healthy and tasty snack!

Nutrition Value:

Calories: 165 | Fat: 9g | Saturates: 3g | Carbs: 18g | Sugars: 11g | Fibre: 2g | Protein: 4g | Salt: 0.14g

SALTY CRUNCHY POPCORN IN AIR FRYER

Preparation Time: 5 minutes | Cooking Time: 8 minutes | Servings: 4 cups

Ingredients:

- Popcorn kernels - 60 grams (¼ cup)
- Olive oil or coconut oil - 1 tablespoon
- Salt, to taste

Instructions:

1. Preheat your air fryer to 200°C (400°F) for about 3 to 5 minutes.
2. Add ¼ cup of popcorn kernels to a medium-sized bowl.
3. Drizzle a tablespoon of olive oil or coconut oil over the popcorn kernels and stir well.
4. Transfer the popcorn to the air fryer basket and spread it out evenly.
5. Close the air fryer basket and set the timer for 6 to 8 minutes. Keep an eye on the popcorn as it cooks, and listen for the popping sounds. If the popping sounds slow down significantly, it's a good sign that the popcorn is almost done.
6. Once the popping has slowed down significantly, carefully open the air fryer basket and use a pair of tongs or oven mitts to remove the basket from the air fryer. Be careful not to burn yourself, as the basket will be hot!
7. Season the popcorn with salt to taste and serve immediately.

Cooking Tip: You can also experiment with different seasonings to give your popcorn a unique flavour, such as garlic powder, Parmesan cheese, or chilli powder.

Nutrition Value:

Calories: 120 | Fat: 4g | Saturates: 1.4g | Carbs: 19g | Sugars: 0g | Fibre: 3g | Protein: 2g | Salt: 0.29g

AIR FRYER ROASTED CASHEWS

Preparation Time: 5 minutes | Cooking Time: 7 minutes | Servings: 2

Ingredients:

- Raw cashews - 280 grams (2 cups)
- Olive oil - 2 tablespoons
- Garlic powder - 1 teaspoon
- Lemon pepper -1 teaspoon
- Sea salt - 1 teaspoon

Instructions:

1. Preheat your air fryer to 160°C (320°F) for 5 minutes.
2. Toss the cashews with olive oil in a mixing bowl until the cashews are well coated.
3. Sprinkle the garlic powder, lemon powder, and sea salt over the cashews and mix well to season evenly.
4. Pour the seasoned cashews into the air fryer basket and air fry for 3 minutes.
5. Open the air fryer basket and shake it to ensure even cooking.
6. Return the basket to the air fryer for 2 to 4 more minutes until the cashews are golden brown and crispy.
7. Check the cashews for doneness and adjust the cooking time as needed.
8. Once the cashews are ready, remove them from the air fryer and let them cool for a few minutes.
9. Serve the crunchy, delicious roasted cashews as a snack or use them in your favourite recipes!

Nutrition Value:

Calories: 399 | Fat: 32g | Saturates: 6g | Carbs: 22g | Sugars: 3g | Fibre: 2g | Protein: 1g | Salt: 0.91g

CHEWY GRANOLA BARS IN AIR FRYER

Preparation Time: 3 minutes | Cooking Time: 15 minutes | Servings: 6

Ingredients:

- Gluten-Free Oats - 250 grams
- Melted Butter - 60 grams
- Brown Sugar - 30 grams
- Honey - 3 tablespoons
- Medium apple, peeled and cooked - 1
- Olive Oil - 1 tablespoon
- Vanilla Essence - 1 tablespoon
- Cinnamon - 1 teaspoon
- Raisins - a handful

Instructions:

1. Begin by blending the gluten-free oats in a blender until smooth. Then, add the rest of the dry ingredients to the blender and blend everything until fully combined.
2. Add all of the wet ingredients to your air fryer baking pan and stir them together using a small wooden spoon. Make sure everything is well combined.
3. Pour the dry ingredients out of the blender and into the baking pan with the wet ingredients. Use a fork to mix everything until there are no lumps.
4. Add the raisins to the mixture and stir them in gently. Then, use a spatula or the back of a spoon to press down the mixture into the baking pan.
5. Preheat your air fryer to 160°C (320°F) for 5 minutes. Once preheated, place the baking pan inside and cook the granola bars for 10 minutes.
6. After 10 minutes, increase the temperature to 180°C (360°F) and cook for 5 more minutes. Check the granola bars for doneness and adjust the cooking time as needed.
7. Once the granola bars reach your desired level of doneness, remove the baking pan from the air fryer and let it cool for a few minutes. Then, place the pan in the freezer for about 5 minutes to let the mixture stiffen.
8. Once stiffened, remove the pan from the freezer and chop the mixture into chewy granola bars of your desired size.
9. Snack on your delicious homemade granola bars!

Nutrition Value:

Calories: 320 | Fat: 13g | Saturates: 5g | Carbs: 46g | Sugars: 17g | Fibre: 5g | Protein: 5g | Salt: 0.76g

LOW CARB AIR FRYER KALE CHIPS

Preparation Time: 3 minutes | Cooking Time: 5 minutes | Servings: 4

Ingredients:

- Kale rinsed and dried - 1 bunch
- Olive or avocado oil - 1 tablespoon
- Salt - ¼ teaspoon

Instructions:

1. Begin by preheating your air fryer to 175°C (350°F) for around 3 minutes.
2. While the air fryer is heating up, prepare the kale by removing the ribs and tearing the leaves into bite-sized pieces (around 1-2 inches in size).
3. Keep the kale leaves in a large mixing bowl.
4. Drizzle the kale leaves with oil and sprinkle with salt. Use your hands or a spoon to toss everything together until all the kale leaves are coated in oil and seasoning.
5. Transfer half the kale leaves to the air fryer basket in a single layer. You will need to work in two batches.
6. Cook for 4 to 5 minutes, shaking the basket halfway through to ensure even cooking. Be sure to keep a close eye on the kale leaves after the 3-minute mark, as they will start to crisp up quickly!
7. Once the first batch is done, remove the kale leaves from the air fryer and transfer them to a serving bowl or plate.
8. Repeat the cooking process with the remaining kale leaves.
9. Once all the kale leaves are cooked and crispy, sprinkle them with additional salt or seasonings if desired.
10. Serve and enjoy your delicious, crispy air-fried kale chips!

Cooking Tip:

- You can store these low-carb kale chips in a paper bag or a plastic bag with a paper towel at room temperature for up to one week. However, their optimal freshness is within the first 2-3 days as they tend to lose their crunchiness over time.
- If your kale chips become soft, you can easily restore their crispness using your air fryer. Preheat the air fryer to 150°C (300°F) and then pop the chips in for 1 to 2 minutes until they are crispy again.

Nutrition Value:

Calories: 40 | Fat: 4g | Saturates: 1g | Carbs: 1g | Sugars: 1g | Fibre: 2g | Protein: 1g | Salt: 0.13g

AIR FRIED MINI PIZZA IN EGGPLANT

Preparation Time: 15 minutes | Cooking Time: 20 minutes | Servings: 4

Ingredients:

- Large eggplant - 1
- Tomato sauce - 240 ml (1 cup)
- Shredded mozzarella cheese - 113 grams (1 cup)
- Sliced black olives - 60 grams (½ cup)
- Chopped fresh basil - 10 grams (¼ cup)
- Salt and pepper, to taste
- Olive oil spray
- Parmesan, oregano, etc (optional)

Instructions:

1. Preheat your air fryer to 190°C (375°F).
2. Wash the eggplant thoroughly and cut it into ½-inch thick slices.
3. Lightly salt both sides of the eggplant slices and place them on a paper towel for 5 minutes. This will help to remove any excess moisture from the eggplant.
4. After 10 minutes, pat the eggplant slices dry with a paper towel.
5. Spray the eggplant slices with olive oil spray on both sides.
6. Place the eggplant slices in the air fryer basket, making sure that they are not overlapping.
7. Air fry the eggplant slices for 5 to 7 minutes or until slightly tender.
8. Remove the eggplant slices from the air fryer and place them on a baking sheet.
9. Spread a tablespoon of tomato sauce on each eggplant slice.
10. Generously sprinkle shredded mozzarella cheese over the tomato sauce.
11. Add sliced black olives on top of the cheese.
12. Sprinkle chopped fresh basil on top of the olives and season with salt and pepper.
13. Place the baking sheet with the eggplant pizzas back in the air fryer.
14. Air fry for 5 to 7 more minutes or until the cheese melts and bubbles.

Nutrition Value:

Calories: 120 | Fat: 7g | Saturates: 3g | Carbs: 9g | Sugars: 5g | Fibre: 4g | Protein: 7g | Salt: 0.32g

AIR FRYER CRISPY POTATO CHIPS

Preparation Time: 10 minutes | Cooking Time: 10 minutes | Servings: 4

Ingredients:

- Large potatoes - 3
- Olive oil - 1 tablespoon
- Salt
- Seasoning of your choice (paprika, garlic powder, onion powder, etc.)

Instructions:

1. Wash the potatoes thoroughly and slice them into thin rounds using a mandoline slicer or a sharp knife. Slice the potatoes as thinly and evenly as possible to ensure they cook evenly.
2. Soak the potato slices in cold water for around 30 minutes. This will help to remove excess starch and make the chips crispier.
3. Drain the water from the potato slices and pat them dry with a paper towel.
4. In a large bowl, toss the potato slices with a tablespoon of olive oil until they are coated evenly.
5. Add salt and seasoning of your choice (if desired) to the potato slices and toss again to evenly distribute the seasoning.
6. Preheat the air fryer to 190°C (375°F).
7. Spread the potato slices in a single layer in the air fryer basket. You may need to do them in batches depending on the size of your air fryer.
8. Air fry the potato slices for 10 to 12 minutes or until golden brown and crispy, flipping them over halfway through cooking.
9. Remove the potato chips from the air fryer basket and place them on a paper towel to cool and drain excess oil.
10. Repeat the process with the remaining potato slices, if needed.
11. Serve the air fryer potato chips as a snack, and enjoy!

Nutrition Value:

Calories: 147 | Fat: 4g | Saturates: 1g | Carbs: 26g | Sugars: 1g | Fibre: 3g | Protein: 3g | Salt: 0.15g

AIR-FRIED KETO CHOCO CHIP COOKIES

Preparation Time: 15 minutes | Cooking Time: 10 minutes | Servings: 12-16

Ingredients:

- Large potatoes - 3
- Olive oil - 1 tablespoon
- Salt
- Seasoning of your choice (paprika, garlic powder, onion powder, etc.)

Instructions:

1. Whisk the almond flour, granulated stevia, salt, and baking soda in a large mixing bowl.
2. In a different bowl, blend the melted coconut oil, egg, and vanilla extract until well combined.
3. Add in the wet ingredients into the dry ingredients and mix until a dough forms.
4. Incorporate the keto-friendly chocolate chips until they are distributed evenly throughout the dough.
5. Cover the dough with plastic wrap and refrigerate it for at least 10 minutes to allow it to firm up.
6. Preheat your air fryer to 175°C (350°F).
7. Meanwhile, scoop out a tablespoon of cookie dough and form the cookies.
8. Place the cookies onto the parchment paper in the air fryer basket, leaving space between each one.
9. Air fry the cookies for 8 to 10 minutes or until they are golden brown on the outside and soft on the inside. If your air fryer does not have a baking tray or basket with a mesh bottom, you may need to flip the cookies over halfway through cooking to ensure they cook evenly.
10. Once the cookies are ready, remove them from the air fryer basket and let them cool on a wire rack for a few minutes.
11. Bite into your delicious keto chocolate chip cookies!

Nutrition Value:

Calories: 118 | Fat: 11g | Saturates: 6g | Carbs: 4g | Sugars: 0g | Fibre: 2g | Protein: 3g | Salt: 0.75g

SAVOURY BEEF JERKY IN AIR FRYER

Preparation Time: 15 minutes | Cooking Time: 10 minutes | Servings: 12-16

Ingredients:

- Inside round steak, thinly stripped - 455 grams (1 pound)
- Soy sauce - 60 ml (¼ cup)
- Worcestershire sauce - 2 tablespoons
- Honey - 1 tablespoon
- Garlic powder - 1 teaspoon
- Onion powder - 1 teaspoon
- Black pepper - ½ teaspoon

Instructions:

1. Begin by freezing the steak for at least 30 minutes until it is firm.
2. Once the steak is firm, use a sharp knife to slice it as thinly as possible, preferably no thicker than ¼ inch.
3. In a large bowl, mix all of the ingredients for the marinade, including the soy sauce, Worcestershire sauce, honey, garlic powder, onion powder, black pepper, and any other spices or flavourings you prefer.
4. Add the sliced steak to the bowl and mix well, ensuring each piece is well-coated.
5. Cover the bowl with plastic wrap or a lid and place it in the refrigerator to marinate for at least one hour or overnight if you can wait. This will allow the flavours to penetrate the meat and make it more tender.
6. Once the meat has marinated, take it out from the refrigerator and arrange the stripes on the racks of your air fryer. You can overlap the strips slightly, but be careful not to stack them on top of each other, as this will prevent even dehydration.
7. Select the "Dehydrate" setting on your Air Fryer and set the temperature to 55°C (130°F).
8. If you have overlapped the meat strips, rotate them or move them around on the racks after 30 minutes to ensure even dehydration.
9. Dehydrate the meat for 60 to 90 minutes or until it is dried and chewy in texture. The exact time will depend on the thickness of the meat strips and the humidity of your environment.
10. Remove the dehydrated beef from the air fryer and let it cool completely before enjoying.

Cooking Tip: You can store the beef jerky in an airtight container or resealable bags to keep it fresh for up to several weeks.

Nutrition Value:

Calories: 110 | Fat: 3g | Saturates: 1g | Carbs: 2g | Sugars: 1g | Fibre: 1g | Protein: 18g | Salt: 0.84g

DESSERTS

RICH CHOCOLATE CAKE IN AIR FRYER

Preparation Time: 20 minutes | Cooking Time: 25 minutes | Servings: 6-8

Ingredients:

- Granulated sugar - 200 grams (1 cup)
- All-purpose flour - ¾ cup (95 grams) plus 2 tablespoons
- Unsweetened cocoa powder - (50 grams) ½ cup
- Baking powder - 1 teaspoon
- Baking soda - ½ teaspoon
- Kosher salt - ½ teaspoon
- Large egg - 1
- Buttermilk - 120 ml (½ cup)
- Vegetable oil - 60 ml (¼ cup)
- Vanilla extract - 1 teaspoons
- Boiling water - 120 ml (½ cup)

Instructions:

1. Preheat the air fryer to 175°C (350°F).
2. Spray the inside of a 7-inch air fryer-safe cake pan with cooking oil.
3. Cut a 9-inch round piece of parchment paper and line the bottom of the pan, making sure it folds up the sides a bit. Spray the parchment paper with more oil and set aside.
4. In a large bowl, whisk together the sugar, flour, cocoa powder, baking powder, baking soda, and salt.
5. Add the egg, buttermilk, vegetable oil, and vanilla extract to the dry ingredients. Mix for 2 minutes until well combined.
6. Gradually stir in the boiling water to create a thin batter.
7. Pour the batter into the prepared pan.
8. Place the pan in the air fryer basket and cook for 25 minutes or until the cake is baked through. Test by inserting a toothpick; there should be no crumbs on it.
9. Allow the chocolate cake to cool in the pan for 10 minutes.
10. Remove the cake from the pan and place it on a wire rack to cool.
11. Decorate with frosting and sprinkles, if desired.
12. Indulge yourself in the rich and decadent chocolate cake!

Nutrition Value:

Calories: 269 | Fat: 11g | Saturates: 1g | Carbs: 41g | Sugars: 34g | Fibre: 1g | Protein: 3g | Salt: 0.34g

HOMEMADE CANNOLI IN AIR FRYER

Preparation Time: 10 minutes | Total Time: 3 hours | Servings: 20

Ingredients:

For the filling:

- Ricotta - 1 (450 g) container
- Mascarpone cheese - 120 grams (½ cup)
- Powdered sugar - 50 grams (½ cup)
- Heavy cream - 180 grams (¾ cup)

- Vanilla extract - 1 teaspoon
- Orange zest - 1 teaspoon
- Kosher salt - ¼ teaspoon
- Mini chocolate chips - for garnish

For the shells:

- Flour - 250 grams (2 cups), plus more
- Granulated sugar - 50 grams (¼ cups)
- Kosher salt - 1 teaspoon
- Cinnamon - ½ teaspoon
- Cold butter, cubed - 4 tablespoons

- White wine - 6 tablespoons.
- Large egg - 1
- Egg white - 1
- Vegetable oil, for frying

Instructions:

MAKE THE FILLING:

1. Drain the ricotta with a fine mesh strainer, and refrigerate it for an hour.
2. Using a hand mixer, beat the heavy cream and ¼ cup powdered sugar in a bowl.
3. Combine the drained ricotta, mascarpone, remaining ¼ cup powdered sugar, vanilla, orange zest, and salt in another large bowl. Fold in the whipped cream, then refrigerate it for at least an hour.

MAKE THE SHELLS:

1. Take a mixing bowl, and whisk the flour, sugar, salt, and cinnamon. Cut the butter into the mixture with your hands or a pastry cutter until pea-sized.
2. Add the wine and egg, and mix until a dough forms. Knead the dough a few times in the bowl to help it come together. Pat into a flat circle, wrap in plastic wrap, and refrigerate for at least an hour or overnight.
3. On a lightly floured surface, divide the dough in half, and roll one half out to ⅛" thickness. Cut out circles using a 4" circle cookie cutter. Repeat with the remaining dough, and re-roll scraps to cut a few extra circles.
4. Wrap the dough around cannoli moulds, and seal the edges with egg whites.

AIR FRY:

1. Working in batches, place moulds in the basket of the air fryer and cook at 175°C (350°F) for 12 minutes or until golden.
2. When the cannolis are cool, gently remove the twist shells off the moulds.
3. Put the filling in a pastry bag fitted with an open star tip. Now pipe it into shells, and dip the ends in mini chocolate chips.
4. Sink your teeth into the crispy shell and creamy filling of your air fried cannoli!

Nutrition Value:

Calories: 239 | Fat: 15g | Saturates: 8g | Carbs: 21g | Sugars: 9g | Fibre: 1g | Protein: 5g | Salt: 0.15g

AIR FRYER CHEESECAKE
WITH GRAHAM CRACKER CRUST

Preparation Time: 10 minutes | Cooking Time: 35 minutes | Servings: 8

Ingredients:

- Salted butter - 6 tablespoons, plus more for greasing the pan
- Graham crackers, finely crushed - 138 grams (1¼ cups)
- Cream cheese, softened - 680 grams (24 ounces)
- Large eggs - 2
- Sweetened condensed milk - 1 (415ml) can
- Pure vanilla extract - 1 teaspoon
- Cherry pie filling - 1 (790 gram) can (optional)

Instructions:

1. Begin by preparing the springform pan for the cheesecake. Brush melted butter on the bottom and sides of a springform pan that fits comfortably in your ninja air fryer.
2. Line the bottom of the pan with parchment paper and then brush it lightly with some melted butter to prevent the cheesecake from sticking.
3. In a medium mixing bowl, blend the graham cracker crumbs and melted butter until the mixture has the texture of a coarse meal.
4. Transfer the graham cracker mixture to the prepared pan and press it evenly with a spoon to form a level crust.
5. Using a stand mixer fitted with the paddle attachment or a hand mixer and a mixing bowl, beat cream cheese, eggs, condensed milk, and vanilla until completely smooth. Take care to scrape the sides and bottom of the bowl occasionally.
6. Put the pan with the crust in the air fryer and pour the cream cheese mixture over it, making sure to leave some space below the rim of the pan.
7. Close the lid of the air fryer and set the air fryer function to bake.
8. Bake the cheesecake at 150°C (300°F) until the top is lightly brown and the centre jiggles slightly. It may take a little more or less time depending on the type of air fryer you are using.
9. Once the cheesecake is baked, carefully remove the springform pan from the air fryer.
10. Let it cool at room temperature for about 1 hour before placing it in the refrigerator for 6 to 8 hours to cool completely.
11. Once the cheesecake is completely cooled, place it on a dish and slice it with a warm knife. Make sure to wipe the knife clean before cuts.
12. If you wish, top the cheesecake with cherry pie filling or your favourite topping.
13. Enjoy the delectable and creamy air fryer cheesecake for a delightful dessert!

Nutrition Value:

Calories: 733 | Fat: 45g | Saturates: 25g | Carbs: 72g | Sugars: 34g | Fibre: 1g | Protein: 12g | Salt: 0.56g

AIR FRIED ADORABLE BERRY HAND PIES

Preparation Time: 10 minutes | Cooking Time: 12 minutes | Servings: 8

Ingredients:

- Store-bought pie crust - 1 box
- Berry jam - 120 ml (½ cup)
- Berries - 75 grams (½ cup)
- Egg white - 1
- Coarse sugar - 2 tablespoons
- Ice cream and additional berries for serving (optional)

Instructions:

1. Begin by preparing the pie crusts. Roll out two pie crusts on a lightly floured surface until they are thin enough to work with.
2. Using a 4-inch circle cutter, cut out fourteen circles from the pie crusts. Take the dough scraps and ball them up. Roll out the dough ball and cut out another two circles.
3. Take eight of the sixteen circles and place two tablespoons of berry jam on top. Then, add a bit of fresh fruit on top of the jam.
4. Brush a thin coat of egg white around the edges of the filled circles to help the top and bottom crusts stick together.
5. Top the filled circles with the remaining unfilled dough circles. Use a fork to crimp the edges together.
6. Pierce the top of each pie once with a fork to allow the steam to escape during baking.
7. Brush the tops of each pie with more of the egg white wash, and sprinkle caster sugar on top of the egg white wash.
8. Preheat your air fryer to 190°C (375°F).
9. Add four of the prepared pies to the air fryer basket tray.
10. Bake the pies for about 12 minutes or until the dough is brown.
11. Serve the pies alone or with ice cream and additional fresh berries on top!

Cooking Tip: You can use any berry jam and fresh berries you want, such as raspberry, blueberry or strawberry jam.

Nutrition Value:

Calories: 306 | Fat: 13g | Saturates: 4g | Carbs: 43g | Sugars: 14g | Fibre: 2g | Protein: 4g | Salt: 14g

MINI PUMPKIN PIES IN AIR FRYER

Preparation Time: 10 minutes | Cooking Time: 8 minutes | Servings: 18

Ingredients:

- Pumpkin - 1 can (425 grams)
- Evaporated milk - 355 ml
- Sugar - 150 grams (¾ cup)
- Salt - ½ teaspoon
- Cinnamon - 1 teaspoon
- Ground ginger - ½ teaspoon
- Ground cloves - ¼ teaspoon
- Eggs - 2
- Mini pie crusts - 18

Instructions:

1. Blend the canned pumpkin, evaporated milk, sugar, salt, cinnamon, ginger, cloves, and eggs in a large mixing bowl.
2. Whisk the ingredients together until you have a smooth and even mixture.
3. Preheat your air fryer to 160°C (320°F) for 5 minutes.
4. Once your air fryer is preheated, place four tins inside the fryer.
5. Use a ¼ cup measuring cup to scoop the filling into the mini pie crusts. Be sure to leave some space at the top of the crusts.
6. Close the air fryer drawer and cook the mini pies at 160°C (320°F) for around 8 minutes. Keep an eye on the pies and remove them once the outer edges firm up. If you add more filling, you may need to cook them for a 1 to 2 more minutes until they are set.
7. Once the mini pies are ready, remove them carefully with tongs and allow them to rest and cool on a cooling rack.
8. Continue the process by adding another batch of four mini pies to the air fryer, and repeat until all the mini pies are cooked.
9. Serve and enjoy your delicious and easy-to-make mini pumpkin pies!

Nutrition Value:

Calories: 66 | Fat: 2g | Saturates: 1g | Carbs: 10g | Sugars: 10g | Fibre: 1g | Protein: 2g | Salt: 0.93g

DELICIOUS AIR FRIED DONUTS

Preparation Time: 1 minutes | Cooking Time: 7 minutes | Servings: 8

Ingredients:

- Self-rising flour - 94 grams (¾ cup)
- Vanilla yoghurt - 245 grams (1 cup)

For the glaze:

- Powdered sugar, sifted - 180 grams (1 ½ cups)
- Water or milk - 1-2 tablespoons
- Rainbow sprinkles - 2 tablespoons (optional)

Instructions:

1. Start by preparing the dough for the doughnuts. In a large mixing bowl, combine the flour and yoghurt and mix well until a thick dough forms.
2. Check the consistency of the dough. If it is too thin, add more flour. If it is too thick, add more yoghurt. Mix well until you get a smooth and pliable dough.
3. Sprinkle some flour onto a clean kitchen surface and transfer the dough onto it. Knead the dough several times until it becomes smooth and elastic.
4. Divide the dough into 8 equal balls, and roll each ball into a long, sausage-like shape.
5. Take each rolled-out piece of dough and connect both ends to form a circular shape, creating a doughnut. Repeat this step until you have 8 doughnuts.
6. Line the air fryer basket with parchment paper to prevent the doughnuts from sticking.
7. Place 2 to 4 doughnuts in the basket, depending on the size of your air fryer. Leave enough space between them to allow room for rising and spreading.
8. Preheat the air fryer to 200°C (400°F) and air fry the doughnuts for 7 to 8 minutes, or until they are firm and golden brown on the outside. You may need to adjust the cooking time depending on your air fryer and the size of the doughnuts.
9. Once the doughnuts are ready, remove them from the air fryer and let them cool completely.
10. While the doughnuts are cooling, prepare the glaze. Sift the powdered sugar into a large bowl, add 1 to 2 tablespoons of water or milk, and stir until a thick, smooth glaze forms.
11. Once the doughnuts have cooled, dip each doughnut into the glaze and place them on a wire rack to allow the excess glaze to drip off.
12. If you want, add sprinkles to the doughnuts for extra decoration. Enjoy your homemade air fryer doughnuts!

Nutrition Value:

1 donut: Calories: 125 | Fat: 2g | Saturates: 1g | Carbs: 19g | Sugars: 3g | Fibre: 1g | Protein: 5g | Salt: 0.21g

BAKED APPLES IN AIR FRYER

Preparation Time: 15 minutes | Cooking Time: 5 minutes | Servings: 4

Ingredients:

- Medium apples - 4
- Lemon juice - 1 tablespoon
- Spray oil

- Coconut whipped cream, regular whipped cream, ice cream or a dollop of yoghurt, for garnishing

For the filling:

- Coconut oil - 3 tablespoons
- Date paste - 4 tablespoons
- Cinnamon, ground - 1 teaspoon
- Nutmeg, ground - ¼ teaspoon

- Plain dried oatmeal - 28 grams (⅓ cup)
- Pecans, chopped - 2 tablespoons
- Raisins - 1 tablespoon

Instructions:

1. Preheat the air fryer to 176°C (350°F).
2. In a microwavable dish, add the coconut oil and date paste. Microwave it for 20 to 30 seconds on high power, just enough to soften.
3. Add cinnamon, nutmeg, dried oatmeal, chopped pecans and raisins and stir until incorporated. Set it aside.
4. Wash the apples and cut a circle around the stem to core them. Be careful not to puncture the sides or poke holes in the bottom of the apple. You can use a melon baller to scoop out the seeds and core.
5. Next, drizzle the inside of the apple with lemon juice.
6. Repeat the process with the remaining apples.
7. Scoop the oatmeal date nut filling into each prepared apple. Make sure to pack the filing with your fingers or a spoon so there are no gaps.
8. Line your air fryer basket or baking tray with either parchment paper or aluminium foil and spray with oil.
9. Place the stuffed apples in the lined air fryer basket or baking tray, leaving some space between each apple.
10. Air fry the stuffed apples for approximately 15 to 18 minutes or until you can easily pierce a knife into the apple. The goal is to have a "crisp but tender apple". If you want your apples to be softer, continue cooking for a few minutes longer.
11. Garnish with coconut cream whipped topping or topping of choice, and dust with some ground cinnamon.
12. Satisfy your sweet tooth guilt-free with these delicious and healthy baked apples for dessert!

Nutrition Value:

1 apple: Calories: 270 | Fat: 15g | Saturates: 9g | Carbs: 39g | Sugars: 25g | Fibre: 6g | Protein: 2g | Salt: 0.04g

SIMPLE LEMON CAKE IN AIR FRYER

Preparation Time: 5 minutes | Cooking Time: 25 minutes | Servings: 8

Ingredients:

- All-purpose flour - 120 grams
- Soft butter - 75 grams
- Margarine - 75 grams
- Eggs - 2
- Fine granulated sugar - 75 grams
- Lemon juice - 2 tablespoons
- Baking powder - 1½ teaspoon
- Vanilla extract - 1 teaspoon
- Salt, a pinch

Instructions:

1. Turn on the air fryer and set the temperature to 16°C (320°F). Let it preheat for 5 minutes.
2. Combine butter, margarine, vanilla extract, and sugar in a large mixing bowl. Use a mixer or whisk to beat the mixture until it becomes light and creamy, which should take about 5 minutes. Be sure not to overmix!
3. Add the eggs one by one, beating each egg into the butter before adding the next.
4. Then, add the flour, baking powder, lemon juice, and a pinch of salt to the mixture. Sift the flour and baking powder together to ensure there are no lumps.
5. Take some soft butter and spread it on the inside of the cake pan to prevent the cake from sticking.
6. Cut a circle of parchment paper and place it at the bottom of the pan.
7. Pour the batter into the cake pan and smooth it out with a spatula. Be sure not to overfill the pan as the cake will rise during baking, and you don't want it to overflow.
8. Put the cake pan in the air fryer basket and slide it into the air fryer.
9. Set the air fryer timer for 25 minutes.
10. After 20 minutes, stick a toothpick into the centre of the cake. If it comes out clean, you can take out the cake from the air fryer. If not, allow it to continue baking for a few more minutes.
11. Once the cake bakes, allow it to cool in the pan for at least 5 minutes.
12. Then, turn the cake pan over onto a wire rack to cool completely.
13. Once the cake has cooled, you can dust it with icing sugar or decorate it with your favourite frosting.
14. Serve your lemon cake with fresh fruit or whipped cream for a delicious dessert. Enjoy!

Nutrition Value:

Calories: 179 | Fat: 9g | Saturates: 5g | Carbs: 21g | Sugars: 10g | Fibre: 0g | Protein: 3g | Salt: 0.67g

FRENCH CREAM PUFFS IN AIR FRYER

Preparation Time: 10 minutes | Cooking Time: 10 minutes | Servings: 24

Ingredients:

- Milk - 100 ml
- Water - 100 ml
- Large eggs - 3
- Butter - 100 grams (3½ oz)

For the filling:

- Heavy cream - 200 ml

- All-purpose flour - 100 grams (3½ ounces)
- Salt - a pinch
- Powdered sugar, for sprinkling

- Sugar - 1 tablespoon

Instructions:

1. In a medium-sized saucepan, add milk, water, butter, and salt. Stir the ingredients using a wooden spoon until the butter completely dissolves in the liquid. Keep stirring the mixture and heat it on medium heat until it just starts to boil. Make sure not to boil the mixture.
2. Once the mixture starts boiling, remove the saucepan from the heat and add the flour. Mix the flour and liquid thoroughly until the dough forms.
3. Put the saucepan back on medium heat and continue stirring the dough for 2 to 3 minutes, baking it in the pan while stirring. The dough should form a ball and not stick to the pan. Once done, remove the pan from the heat and transfer the dough to a large bowl. Stir the dough again and let it cool for 3 to 5 minutes.
4. Add the eggs to the dough one at a time. Stir the dough thoroughly with each addition of an egg and let it completely incorporate before adding the next egg.
5. Preheat your Air Fryer to 180°C (360°F) for 3 minutes.
6. Fill the dough into a piping bag using a spatula or spoon. Pipe little heaps of dough on the air fryer grilling pan, slightly flattening the tops of the piped dough.
7. Place the grilling pan into the air fryer and cook the puffs for 10 minutes or until golden brown. When you tap the bottom of the puffs, they should produce a hollow sound.
8. Once the puffs bake, let them cool on a wire rack.
9. Pour the heavy cream into a mixing bowl, add sugar, and whip it until stiff.
10. With the same piping bag, fill the puffs from the bottom with the whipped cream.
11. Sprinkle some powdered sugar over the cream-filled puffs before serving.
12. Indulge in the delectable and fluffy goodness of the cream puffs, satisfying your sweet cravings with every bite!

Nutrition Value:

Calories: 106 | Fat: 7g | Saturates: 4g | Carbs: 9g | Sugars: 6g | Fibre: 0g | Protein: 2g | Salt: 0.42g

AIR FRIED NUTELLA LAVA CAKES

Preparation Time: 10 minutes | Cooking Time: 10 minutes | Servings: 2

Ingredients

- Semi-sweet chocolate chips - 120 grams (½ cup)
- Butter - 4 tablespoons
- Eggs - 2

- Vanilla extract - 1 teaspoon
- Salt - ¼ teaspoon
- All-purpose flour - 3 tablespoons
- Powdered sugar - 50 grams (½ cup)

For the Nutella filling:

- Nutella - 2 tablespoons
- Butter, softened - 1 tablespoon

- Powdered sugar - 1 tablespoon

Instructions:

1. Preheat your air fryer to 180°C (360°F).
2. Take a medium-sized microwave-safe bowl and add chocolate chips and butter.
3. Heat the bowl in the microwave for 30-second increments, stirring the mixture during each interval, until the chocolate chips and butter are completely melted and smooth.
4. Add eggs, vanilla, salt, flour, and powdered sugar to the bowl with the melted chocolate chip mixture. Whisk briskly to combine the ingredients thoroughly.
5. In a separate bowl, mix Nutella, softened butter, and powdered sugar until well combined.
6. Prepare the ramekins by spraying them with oil.
7. Fill each ramekin halfway with the chocolate chip mixture.
8. Then, add half of the Nutella filling in the centre of each ramekin.
9. Cover the Nutella filling with the remaining chocolate chip mixture.
10. Carefully place the ramekins in the preheated air fryer and cook for 8 to 11 minutes.
11. Once the cooking is complete, carefully remove the ramekins from the air fryer and allow them to cool for 5 minutes.
12. Use a butter knife to run around the edges of the cake, gently loosening it from the sides of the ramekin. Flip it out onto a serving plate.
13. Top the cake with your desired toppings, such as ice cream, chocolate syrup, or any other delicious treats you might like.
14. Indulge in the rich and gooey chocolate lava cake filled with creamy Nutella!

Nutrition Value:

Calories: 776 | Fat: 51g | Saturates: 32g | Carbs: 77g | Sugars: 62g | Fibre: 4g | Protein: 10g | Salt: 0.58g

FINAL WORDS

Cooking was never this easy before one could lay their hands on a trusted air fryer. The Ninja Air Fryer has many features that you can count on every day. This means that you will always have options when it comes to cooking and giving yourself or your family some variety in their regular meals. We hope you love this cooking journey with our Ninja Air Fryer Cookbook and have learned a few things from it. Choose any recipe you need to go for according to your craving and preference, as this book has unlimited options for you to try out. The best thing about this cookbook is that you will never find yourself stuck with the question of what to cook today, as you can lay your hands on multiple dishes that you can prepare whenever you feel like it in no time.

There is no other ease in today's world than finding an easy-to-go solution for cooking because we all need to save as much time and energy as possible. With this book, everything can go smoothly, as you will find many options to try out that will enhance your culinary skills and help you do everything in the best way possible. Try out your favourite dishes from the ones we have gathered here in this book for you, and let us know about your cooking experience. We would love to learn more about your favourite dishes and what you like about this book. Thank you for being with us throughout the book!

Printed in Great Britain
by Amazon

33168260R00057